RADICAL

ALSO BY NICHOLAS VON HOFFMAN

A Devil's Dictionary of Business
Hoax
Citizen Cohen
Organized Crimes (fiction)

RADICAL

A Portrait of Saul Alinsky

Nicholas von Hoffman

NATION
BOOKS
New York

Nation Books is a co-publishing venture of the Nation Institute and
the Perseus Books Group.

Books published by Nation Books are available at special discounts for
bulk purchases in the United States by corporations, institutions, and
other organizations. For more information, please contact the Special
Markets Department at the Perseus Books Group, 2300 Chestnut
Street, Suite 200, Philadelphia, PA 19103, or call (800) 810-4145, ext.
5000, or e-mail special.markets@perseusbooks.com.

Designed by Timm Bryson

Library of Congress Cataloging-in-Publication Data

von Hoffman, Nicholas.
    Radical : a portrait of Saul Alinsky / Nicholas von Hoffman.
    p. cm.
    ISBN 978-1-56858-439-3 (alk. paper)
    1. Alinsky, Saul David, 1909–1972. 2. Radicals—United States—
Biography. 3. Social reformers—United States—Biography. 4. Political
activists—United States—Biography. 5. Community organization—
United States—History—20th century. I. Title.
    HN90.R3A6579 2010
    303.48'4092—dc22
    [B]
                                    2010003847
10 9 8 7 6 5 4 3 2 1

To Esme and Gregory

"The sleeping are coworkers and fabricators of the things that happen in the world. . . . To those that are awake there is one world in common, but of those that are asleep, each is withdrawn to a private world of his own. . . . The people must fight for their law as for their walls."

—HERACLITUS, ONE OF SAUL'S FAVORITE WRITERS

ACKNOWLEDGMENTS

Many thanks to Susan Dooley Carey who fine-combed the manuscript and rearranged it to give it the appearance of a book. As many thank-yous go to Sanford Horwitt, Alinsky's biographer, for hours of discussion, innumerable suggestions and much encouragement and the same to Lester Hunt for his generosity. Thanks also to my editor, Carl Bromley, who thought up this project and sped it along with intelligent guidance, editorial acuity and cheerful encouragement. Gratitude to my agent, Mary Evans, for her robust representation and suggestions for improving the manuscript. Many warm thanks also to Irene Alinsky, Saul's widow. To my son Alexander, my gratitude for his insights, his erudition and for listening to his old man gabble on about the project.

I am also in debt to a number of people who were good enough to give of their time and intelligence. Among them are Edward Chambers, Michael Gecan, Arnold Graf, Richard Harmon, Jonathan Lange, Gretchen Laue, Phil Primack and Wade Rathke.

INTRODUCTION

Looking down from Heaven or up from Hell—Saul Alinsky's preferred postmortem abode—he must be pleased. He loved attention and these last couple of years he has been getting it. His books are selling by the thousands, he is being credited with electing a president and hundreds of thousands who had not heard his name five years ago are clogging cyberspace reviling him.

The man who invented community organizing, "the big, laughing, brazen, sensitive, contradictory, gutsy, utterly outlandish head of everything," as Georgie Anne Geyer referred to him, is getting the credit or the blame for being the formative factor in the political development of Barack Obama.

The organizing techniques used by the Obama people in the 2008 Iowa primary, which changed Obama from a long shot to a serious candidate, are supposed to have been copied from Alinsky. He is also blamed for having put a drop of his power elixir into the goblet of President Obama's secretary of state, Hillary Rodham Clinton, who wrote her senior college thesis about his work. Were you to listen to their enemies, you'd believe that the number of Washington politicians who have drunk Saul's Kool-Aid grows by the month.[1]

Even right-wingers are following his lead. Those who have taken to breaking up town hall meetings with their disruptive shouting have read or misread Alinsky's book of tactics with the same assiduity as the Left. Were Saul alive he would delight in this hurly-burly. He thrived on days of tumult and nights of stress. He would have liked to have been a legend in his own time, but becoming one forty years after his death must be a satisfaction to his mischievous spirit.

If historians dwell on how much of an influence Alinsky had in the election of the first African American president they may overlook his less visible but more durable contributions. Directly and indirectly through countless organizations which spring from him he taught millions of Americans that their best and only chance of determining their lives is by organization. From him they learned that a large crowd flashing slogans on cardboard signs and demonstrating on the Mall or being dragged off by the police at an occasional sit-in cannot substitute for the power of lasting organization.

Without power, he explained, nothing can be done, no rock moved, no law written, no wrong righted. Power, Alinsky taught, comes in two forms only: money and people. If you have the money you don't need people. Without money the way to power is to organize the people.

Organization was an Alinsky specialty, as were tactics at which he was infernally creative. He was so good at them that some people mistakenly take him to be an amoral figure whose major accomplishment was the perfection of tactical monkeyshines. Through the medium of the Industrial Areas Foundation (IAF) which he began and other entities which he inspired, scores of organizations in various shapes and forms have built hundreds of thousands of homes for low-income people even as they have protected civil liberties, achieved a living wage for countless workers, gotten jobs, paved streets and schooled children. In the aggregate millions have helped themselves by banding together.

Like the heirs of the Prophet, Alinsky's legatees squabble over the true meaning of the master's teachings. How ironic are these arguments about one of the least-dogmatic and most flexible of men. Alinsky believed that liberty was to be redefined and rewon by every generation according to its circumstances and the demands of its time. The constant was not this or that method or these or those tactics; the constant was democracy, a form of government as arduous to keep as it is to gain. That was Alinsky's life work.

This book is not biography or an exegesis on his thinking. It is an *homage*, a portrait of Alinsky by someone who knew him well and loved him. There are only three or four of us still living.

A word of note: The quotes attributed to a published source can be considered accurate. Those without attribution are the author's best recollection of things said a very long time ago.

ONE

MY BLUNDERING ATTEMPTS TO ORGANIZE; MEETING SAUL
AND BEING HIRED; APPRENTICESHIP IN THE URBAN
WILDERNESS; WHAT IT IS AN ORGANIZER DOES AND WHY
ONE WOULD EVER TRY TO DO IT; WHERE ALINSKY CAME
FROM AND HOW HE WAS SHAPED; OUR SHARED OPINION OF
THE RICH AND TOO POWERFUL

If the ends don't justify the means, what does?

—SAUL ALINSKY

At the time I first met Saul Alinsky, circa the summer of 1953, I was twenty-two years old and believed that I had my impulses for saving the human race under control. I was involved not with Saul, whom I had not yet met, but with one of his favorite authors, Alexis de Tocqueville. I was trying to write a radio dramatization of the Frenchman's visit to America for a high-minded appendage to the University of Chicago, the name of which I've forgotten. My knowledge of the world or anything else was blotchy at

1

best. My outstanding trait was talking, which I did not well but often.

With my wife and small son I was living in a dingy neighborhood on Chicago's South Side, an area that had seen a recent influx of Puerto Rican immigrants. Though most of the residents would have liked to kick them back out that was not possible, so they took them for every penny they were able to cheat, trick or con the new arrivals out of.

Rene and Yolanda, a flamboyant Cuban couple who ran a little restaurant-cum-bodega, made me see the difficulties facing the newcomers and I took it into my head to organize a mutual self-defense group of some kind. I had no idea exactly what kind since my previous though limited experience was with political organizations and labor unions.

The outcome of these exertions was an entity called El Comité Latino Americano. Although I was highly visible in its formation I cannot claim to have done much organizing. When seen I was roaring around the neighborhood pushing my son in a stroller, flapping my arms and waving my mouth. In so doing I had blundered into a home truth about organizing: Good organizers don't organize. They get other people to do it.

The real organizing was done by Lester Hunt, who spoke fluent Spanish, and Juan Sosa, who worked at the Sherwin-Williams paint plant on the far southeast side of the city. Sosa was proof you do not have to be large and noisy to organize. You could hardly hear him speak.

Lester, working under the auspices of the Episcopalian Church, had spent several years in the mountains of pre-Castro

Cuba teaching the children of poverty-racked peons. When it was time for him to say good-bye the people were too poor to buy him a farewell present, so they made one out of a discarded, rusty railroad spike, which they hand-polished until it gleamed like silver.

We were running a social first-responders service, trying and failing to get people jobs, saving them from landlords or, as we did one morning at 2:00 a.m., extricating them from the police lockup. One of our people had called from the Grand Crossing police station where he and seven or eight of his buddies had been taken after the cops had raided their card game. They were being charged with a first-offense misdemeanor: failure to grease a police palm while engaged in a game of chance.

I in turn called Abner Mikva who would one day become a congressman, a federal appeals court judge and White House counsel during the height of President Bill Clinton's legal troubles. He climbed out of bed without pause or hesitation, the Bill of Rights in hand. It was first light before Ab had gotten the last of our people out of the hoosegow. I did not know that such acts of generosity could not by themselves build an organization. That and other points I would later come to appreciate under Alinsky's tutelage.

Although mostly I banged around trying to make myself understood by drawing on my high school French and speaking in a loud voice, I did know enough Spanish to understand when a panicky and frightened man stopped me on the street and told me his wife was having a baby. I was not to keep congratulating him, he said; I was to come with him. In his cramped third-floor apartment a woman lay on a bed near to giving birth. A semi-circle of frightened children stared at their mother.

I went back downstairs and knocked on the building manager's door. It opened just wide enough and long enough for the woman to hear what the situation was before she slammed it. There was a pay phone in the hall and I called the Chicago Maternity Center and explained the emergency. They said they did not attend to births by mothers not registered with them.

Returning to the apartment, I tried to make the woman comfortable. I indicated I needed boiling water since every frontier doctor in every western movie I had seen had commanded it. I shooed the children away. The water came and while I debated with myself about how to use it, nature did what needed to be done. Several days later I ran into the father and asked him, expecting a small show of gratitude and some recognition of my obstetric skills, what he and his wife had named their little boy.

"Guillermo."

Not long after that I met Saul.

My coming to work for him began with Jack Egan, a smallish, invincibly likable man, a priest who was neither sanctimonious nor preachy. Though Egan spoke in a clipped fashion that made him sound hard, his besetting sin was softness; he lacked the faculty of suspicion and thought far too well of every layperson he met. Church politics was another thing.

He and another priest, Msgr. John O'Grady, had taken an interest in El Comité Latino Americano, providing what little money we had. It was a rickety organization and its lack of funding guaranteed that it was not going to last long. The Latin

American Committee garnered the goodwill and loyalty of the newcomers but the Puerto Ricans did not run it. We auslanders did.

O'Grady and Egan thought some guy I'd never heard of—Saul Alinsky—might be interested enough to step in and save El Comité. Egan arranged for us all to have dinner at the Palmer House Hotel Grill.

With the heaviness of its linens and the muffled clink of its silver, the Grill felt more like the Union League Club than a steakhouse. The man sitting with Egan and O'Grady wore glasses that shielded exophthalmic eyes and his every gray hair was smoothed into place. I had been promised a firecracker but what I was getting was a middle-aged businessman.

Egan invited me to give a description of what we were doing at El Comité. I offered up a picture of the Puerto Rican situation to a blank-faced Alinsky and then described the work of El Comité, omitting only Guillermo.

When I finished and Egan asked Saul what he thought, his answer was, "It's a bucket of shit," a judgment that prompted me to throw my napkin on the table, rise and let loose a speech to the effect that Saul might be tired, over the hill, no longer able or willing to fight the good fight, but I etc., etc. This callow Billingsgate bounced off Saul with no visible effect, although I think while he listened he mistakenly saw in me himself as a young man.

After I had finished, he flipped his hand at me, softly and slowly, indicating I should resume my seat. He repeated exactly what he thought the El Comité was full of and then said he'd give me a job with the proviso I got a haircut and a decent suit. Though the Latin American Committee was not dumped, it was nursed along for some years by others and I went to work for Saul.

Years later he told me that he hired César Chávez and me on the same day, but Chávez had already demonstrated enormous promise. On his first day on the job, Chávez had plenty to do in California putting together the Community Service Organization (CSO), the forerunner of the United Farm Workers. He was an experienced and talented organizer. I, on the other hand, had shown little more than the ability to wave my mouth around. All I had to offer when I reported for work was a haircut and a new suit.

I had no very precise idea what I had been hired to do or be. I have no recollection of the term "community organizer" being used. Saul ordinarily referred to what we were doing as "the work," saying he was going to get business cards printed that would read "Saul Alinsky—Have Trouble, Will Travel." It expressed his attitude of being up for anything the time and circumstances offered.

It may have been that Saul had no idea what to do with me. He had no ongoing organizational drive and probably thought that letting me return to the Comité would have reinforced the bad habit of doing emergency social work in place of laying the foundations of an independent organization. He told me to go out to the Near West Side, find out what was going on—he was no more specific than that—and send in a weekly report containing what I had learned, along with my expense account including all receipts. Under no circumstance was I to call him, turn up at the office or in any other fashion make my existence on the globe known to him. If and when he wished to see me I would be told. Otherwise I was to vanish.

In time I learned about the West Side. The part closest to downtown had become an area of first settlement for African Americans recently come north. They lived in wretched housing under the political suzerainty of the Italian branch of organized crime. Farther to the west they lived in a little better housing under the suzerainty of the Jewish branch of organized crime.

I met ordinary people picking a way through the physical ruins toward a better life. I met small businessmen, real estate agents, city employees, some of whom were showing up for work and making a stab at getting something done. I fell in with a terrified alderman who met me at hamburger stands because he said that his office was bugged by organized crime or "the syndicate" as it was called then. I met another alderman who said nothing of the sort and was later found kneeling, his hands handcuffed and a bullet in the back of his head.

I found Saul's spoor everywhere. My investigative wanderings took me at one point to the rectory of St. Philip Benizi Parish on the Near North Side, across the street from the Cabrini Green Homes public housing project. St. Philip's pastor, Father Luigi Giambastiani, was an Italian from the Old Country known for his views on race. "It is true that some *idealists* dream of an American millennium when all the races will be found fused into one American race," he wrote in a 1922 parish bulletin, "but in the meantime it is good that each think of his own. . . . Italians be united to your churches . . . give your offerings to the Italian churches who need it."[1]

In the early 1940s Saul had used this prejudice to overcome Father Luigi's objection to what would become a prototype for the nightmare of public housing. The priest had clout strong enough at city hall to veto the project, but Saul had sold him on the idea that the new housing would be for Italian people and thus would strengthen the parish.

It had worked out otherwise. Even then, in the early '50s, you risked life and limb if you took an unguarded stroll through Cabrini Green. When I knocked on the rectory door Father Luigi guided me into the dining room, a dark place dominated by a heavy table in Grand Rapids baroque. We sat there drinking tea as he recounted what had happened to his parish. "What's there now? Niggers! Niggers as far as you can see!" he said, pulling aside the heavy drapery. Before making each point he prefaced it with, "You tell Saul" or "You tell your boss" how the people were gone, the slums had come, the school was falling down, the collection plate was empty and the parish was broke.

The latter was of particular importance to Father Luigi, who was the most nickel-nursing miser in the archdiocese. Stories of his avarice provided comic material in rectories all over Chicago. When one of his assistants lay dying, Father Luigi, who had a special cost-cutting arrangement with a local printer, conferred with the doctor on how long the man might live. Twelve to eighteen hours at most, said the doctor. As was the church's custom, a death announcement, elegantly printed on heavy paper with the time and place of the funeral, was rushed through and sent out to the several thousand priests, nuns, brothers and important laymen of the archdiocese. The twelve-hour line was crossed and the assistant still lived. At the eighteenth hour he began to recover. Mourners next received a postcard saying that there had been a hitch and the obsequies were on hold.

After leaving Father Luigi, I ran into Eye-in-the-Sky O'Keefe, a blind bookmaker who practiced his calling a block or so away on Clark Street. I said something about Luigi's money complaints, and Eye-in-the-Sky told me that Father Luigi was anything but broke. The priest had his cancer shrine in a separate nearby building, he reminded me. How could that help, Sky? There couldn't be room for more than seventy-five people in that little place. The rear was much larger, Sky explained, and was consecrated to secular purposes. The back was a warehouse where "the characters" stored their slot machines and other wagering devices, a use of the shrine for which Father Luigi was compensated.

In my wanderings, I also found traces of Saul's doings as a young criminologist when he was studying, if that's the right word, gangsters who were gunfighting up and down Taylor Street. I met men who told me stories of Saul holding some of these young men after they had been shot.

Over the years when people came to Saul to ask, "How do you do it?" he would say, "Start where you are." He was less forthcoming about how a person could find out where that was and if he had talked about the process few would have listened; they were fixed on the starting point. Saul did not tell them that the finding-out part is where the magic is.

Here is the proposition. You are to go to a strange place where you do not know anyone, where you have not been supplied with any contacts, where you will be telling people that you are employed by a funny-sounding organization called the Industrial Areas Foundation, which they have not heard of and which carries no clout or status. You are alone. You are a nobody.

When you have no leverage, nothing to offer in exchange for your intrusion into another person's life, even if that intrusion is only in the form of a few questions, you'd better have a few tap-dancing steps in your repertoire. When I was organizing in a low-income black neighborhood in Chicago, I'd dress to the nines. I'd wear a blue pin-striped suit with a big gold watch on a chunky gold chain in the pocket of the red vest from A. Sulka. I sported a bowler hat and a chesterfield coat. One more flashy detail and I'd have been over the line into pimpdom but as it was I gave the impression of prosperity in a great gray, glum part of a big-city slum. It worked for me. Without saying anything I conveyed the completely false impression that I was in the money and if you listened to what I had to say you might be in it too.

That rig fitted me and the moment. But as Saul repeatedly said, you cannot count on the next organizing situation being like the last one.

The need to adapt to the situation was a lesson Saul learned when he was in graduate school at the University of Chicago and set out around 1931 to study organized crime. There was no reason the mobsters should give him the time of day. But there was one man who told such terrible jokes that others at the table would get up and leave when he said, "Did I tell ya the one about? . . ." Saul made his first friend in the Mob by laughing at this guy's jokes. Although when I first knew Saul I took it for granted that the Palmer House Grill was his favorite restaurant, I later figured out it was the gangster hangout on the city's Near North Side.

It comes to you slowly that before you learn anything about the people into whose midst you have dropped yourself, you are going to have to learn about yourself. Otherwise you will not be able to explain yourself to the people whose cooperation you must gain. Organizing or doing whatever it was Saul had sent me to do on the gangster-ridden Near West Side is not like selling Bibles or vacuum cleaners door-to-door. You cannot flamboozle people with a spiel, make your sale and hop off down the road. You will be coming back. You are building a relationship. You are not the only one who gets to ask the questions; they get to ask them too and you had better have convincing, honest answers.

The unknowable, knowable self is an organizer's greatest aid and worst obstacle. As a stranger from the outside one of the things people want to know about you is why you are doing this. Barack Obama wrote about how he handled or did not handle that question:

> Over the past five years, I've often had a difficult time explain-
> ing my profession to folks. Typical is a remark a public school
> administrative aide made to me one bleak January morning,

while I waited to deliver some flyers to a group of confused and angry parents who had discovered the presence of asbestos in their school.

"Listen, Obama," she began. "You're a bright young man, Obama. You went to college, didn't you?"

I nodded.

"I just cannot understand why a bright young man like you would go to college, get that degree and become a community organizer."

"Why's that?"

"Cause the pay is low, the hours is long, and don't nobody appreciate you." She shook her head in puzzlement as she wandered back to attend to her duties.

I've thought back on that conversation more than once during the time I've organized with the Developing Communities Project, based in Chicago's far south side. Unfortunately, the answers that come to mind haven't been as simple as her question. Probably the shortest one is this: It needs to be done, and not enough folks are doing it.[2]

I had a half-dozen answers to the question of why I was doing this work seven days a week, twelve hours a day, but none that were full and complete because I didn't know myself. Saul would say that he did it because he could not think of anything else that he would rather be doing; if he did, he would go do it. He did it, he said, because he hated bullies. In the 1950s and '60s the work was stormy, exciting and fun because it was a historic time and though we may not have been making history, we were contributing to it. That, as Saul, would point out, is a powerful motive.

Even though Saul would often imply that in me he saw himself as a young man, our backgrounds were totally different. Saul used to say that he was a slum kid. Technically he was since he was born in the Maxwell Street neighborhood of first settlement for Jews. It was the Chicago ghetto, its streets lined with push-carts and the houses crammed with sweatshops. There on Maxwell Street his father had his tailoring establishment but Saul was six when the family moved just to the west into the Lawndale area of the city, which was not a slum then though later it would become one.

Lawndale in Alinsky's childhood was a solid community of Jewish strivers, including his father who prospered to the extent that he was able to buy an apartment building. Saul was the child of his father's second marriage, the first having produced three children. I cannot recall Saul's mentioning his two half-brothers, and if he mentioned his half-sister, it wasn't often. As for his father, there were few words for him and none were flattering to this narrow, limited and meager-spirited man.

Saul's parents, being hardworking and religiously Orthodox, fitted in well in the community but not with each other. Saul was thirteen when they divorced and his father left for Los Angeles where, when his son came to visit, he stashed him in a boardinghouse. There was some benefit to the ostracism; Saul had an affair with a young woman five or six years older than he. As was his habit, he called it "shacking up," but whenever he mentioned his nameless partner, it was with a certain affectionate warmth.

His mother, who was a generation younger than Benjamin Alinsky, went on to have three or possibly more husbands. Saul's biographer, Sanford Horwitt, is uncertain on the point. Saul was devoted to his mother, a woman whom others considered a termagant. Of Sarah's roiling ways he was oblivious. Her Old World views and her Yiddishisms amused her son, and the succession of husband-stepfathers might not have existed as far as I could tell.

As a kid Saul was mad for a radio, one of the miraculous developments of his boyhood years. He sent away for a radio kit that, I believe, cost twenty-five cents, a lot of money for a boy in those years. When it arrived and he opened the box, all that came out was "a crystal and a few wires" to his lasting disillusionment. Forty years later Saul was still talking about how cheated he had felt.

As he grew older Saul traded his enthusiasm for radio for the glamorous career of the period—aviation. He spent his idle hours running errands and helping out at Checkerboard Field, the Chicago base for the country's nascent airmail service. Charles A. Lindbergh flew into Checkerboard on his mail run from St. Louis before he became a world-famous figure.

When Saul was there, the dominant personality at Checkerboard Field was Tony Yackey, pilot, builder of planes and promoter of the new industry. It was for him that Saul ran his errands until, as the *Chicago Daily News* reported, "The crumpling wing of an airplane of his own manufacture late yesterday cut short the career of one of Chicago's pioneers in commercial aviation when Wilfred A. (Tony) Yackey plunged to his death while making a test flight near his factory in Maywood."[3] Saul, who had hoped that Yackey would give him flying lessons, saw him die in the crash. He gave up the idea of flying.

The big events of his growing up were the battles with the Polish boys on the other side of Crawford Avenue, his breaking his leg and spending a year in a plaster cast and the "older woman" at the California boardinghouse.

With the discovery of King Tut's tomb in 1922 mummies seemed to have won the same place in the imagination of American children as dinosaurs have today. Saul was crazy about them and his interest continued into his undergraduate years at the University of Chicago, where his major was archaeology. "I fell in love with the subject. It was all very exciting and dramatic to me. The artifacts were not just pieces of stone and clay. My imagination could carry me back to the past so that when I stood in front of an old Inca altar I could hear the cries of human sacrifices."[4]

Until the Depression hit, Alinsky's interest in democracy and social justice was faint. In his undergraduate days when Calvin Coolidge was president and the stock market was soaring, Saul with a group of classmates brought food to striking miners in southern Illinois. But by his own description questions such as wages and working conditions for industrial workers were not uppermost in his mind.

Other questions were inescapable. In Saul's time anti-Semitism permeated the social life of the University of Chicago, as it did schools everywhere. The Quadrangle Club, then a private organization serving as the school's faculty club, did not admit Jews. When a friend of Saul's invited Saul and his girlfriend to a dance at the club, the friend was threatened with expulsion.

The Depression dried up money for archaeology and for a time Saul got by on his wits and the indulgence of his Swedish landlady. Then he was awarded a fellowship in criminology, one generous enough so that he would be able to earn a doctorate in the field. Somebody up above must have been watching over him. Saul said that he had never applied for the fellowship, that one day it had simply come in the mail from Robert Hutchins, the university's president.

———————

Like Saul's, my parents separated when I was young, but there the similarities ended. My mother was born in Weehawken, New Jersey, in a family with roots in Pennsylvania and Missouri. She was a feminist, a pacifist and if not a socialist, which was too regimented for her, at least a trooper for social justice. Having spent part of her childhood in Hazleton, Pennsylvania, in the anthracite fields, she had seen a little of the battles between the coal miners and the mine owners and had become, like Alinsky, an admirer of John L. Lewis. Of coal mining as an occupation she would say, "They cannot print enough money to pay those men!"

She was, as I used to tell her, the only poor dentist in New York City, poor because she took so many patients who had low-paying or no-paying jobs. She was also a bohemian whose life was chockablock with painters, writers, acupuncturists, vaudevillians, anarchists and one-of-a-kind persons whom there is no way to categorize and no room to describe here.

My father was an ex-czarist officer with political opinions different from my mother's. I was seven years old before I realized that "thegoddamnreds" might not be one word. He made a slender living being an explorer, photographer and adventurer engaged in such things as capturing animals in Australia for American zoos and taking rich men on African safaris.

The adjective "dashing" does not do him justice. Between wars, duels, scrapes and hair-raising escapes it is said that Papa followed a ballet dancer with whom he was smitten from St. Petersburg to Buenos Aires. He spent years in remote places in the Far East and told eye-popping tales about events he was party to across the globe but he suffered from a stage-four Munchausen complex (a disorder of the hyperactive imagination that I may have been the first to isolate). Though others may have, I did not question stories such as his sneaking into a Moroccan seraglio to meet a harem wife who said she had been kidnapped from her native Georgia (then part of Russia) and trundled off to North Africa.

Much of his life revolved around the Explorers Club, where I believe he was the chairman of its entertainment committee. In that capacity he supervised the Safari Dinners at which he fed the membership dishes with names that sounded to me like Hippopotamus Wellington and Anteater Rockefeller. When I was a lad he would take me to the Explorers Club where there was a parrot they said belonged to Amelia Earhart. The frightening animal would take hold of my father's thumb by its beak, and the two of them would go about their business at the club together. On some visits I was brought forward to shake hands with some of America's most famous admirals and generals, which thrill was destroyed as I cringed, watching my father lose his dignity making over the millionaires whose money kept the club going.

Like Saul he understood money is power, but unlike Saul he gave them both unthinking and unreserved deference.

At the other end of the parent continuum my mother struggled to make ends meet, in part because such rich patients as she had made it a point to delay paying their bills for months at a time. One of her patients was Loton Horton, the head of Sheffield Farms, a major dairy supplying milk to New York City. He was sitting in the dentist's chair one day during the Great Depression when he told my mother with considerable satisfaction that he had five "girls" working the switchboard and they all had Ph.D.'s. Mother, who was ordinarily the politest of women, fixed him with her frightening blue eyes and said, "You ought to be ashamed of yourself!"

Saul and I came to our dislike and distrust of the rich by different paths, but it was one thing we had in common.

TWO

O ut on the Near West Side with no boss, no set schedule, no place I had to be, I was burdened with the freedom of puzzling out what to do, which led to asking myself why I was doing it and who I might be. On the West Side I was an outsider, but Saul believed there was a place for the outside organizer. Moses was one of his favorites, Saint Paul another. Saul, a Jewish intellectual from a background vastly different from that of the people he worked with, knew what it's like to play the part of the stranger. Saul believed that although once in a blue moon spontaneous organizational combustion happens and people come together on their own, more often they need the outside person who brings new views of familiar situations and convinces them of the possibility of change. Just any outsider will not do. Saint Paul, the ultimate outsider, came to the non-Jews not only with an appealing message but with a personal history that fitted the moment and special gifts for organization.

When Saul started there was no known social role for somebody calling himself a "community organizer." Fifty years ago you might as well have said that you were a tourist from Alpha Centauri. It would have conveyed the same meaning as introducing one's self as a community organizer. As Barack Obama wrote:

> In 1983, I decided to become a community organizer. There wasn't much detail to the idea; I didn't know anyone making a living that way. When my classmates in college asked me just what it was that a community organizer did, I couldn't answer them directly. Instead, I'd pronounce on the need for change. Change in the White House . . . Change in Congress . . . Change in the mood of the country, manic and self-absorbed. Change won't come from the top, I would say. Change will come from a mobilized grass roots. That's what I'll do, I'll organize black folks. At the grass roots for change.[1]

If organizers cannot tell others what it is they do, it is in part because, though they know what they want to do, they do not know how they are going to do it until they have gotten it done. As Obama said of the work, "Ah, yes. *Real* change. It had seemed like such an attainable goal back in college, an extension of my personal will, and my mother's faith, like boosting my grade point average or giving up liquor; a matter of taking and assigning responsibility. Only now, after a year of organizing, nothing seemed simple."[2]

Besides undersea exploration in a bathysphere few activities are lonelier than parachuting into a place where you have not been before, where you know no one and know little more than the information about the area in the U.S. Census. The lone organizer has no credentials that people might respect, no status in the outside world, no money, no power, no nothing except whatever the ability to work with others, charm, guile and imagination can concoct.

He—or she—is that oft-evoked but seldom-seen figure, the outside agitator. Unless he knows his business, he will agitate the people to organize to throw him out. A couple of missteps and Mr. or Ms. Organizer will look like a stranger who pops in out of nowhere to tell the locals that they are too stupid to take care of their own selves and their own problems.

But gifted outside organizers do have advantages. They come with fresh eyes and new ideas, enabling them to see possibilities those already there may not realize. They can bring hope and excitement because they are not like the people they have come to organize. One of the reasons organizers fail—and many did in Alinsky's time—is that they try to fit in. The more successful they are at fitting in the less they will seem to offer and yet the more they don't fit in the more precarious their position. Getting it right ain't easy.

A half century ago the occupation of community organizer meant nothing. Even after all that has been done since Saul's death and Barack Obama's talking about being one, quondam mayor Rudi Giuliani of New York City could ask, "Just what does a community organizer do?" Unlike many others, Giuliani actually did know the answer. As New York's mayor he had often had to meet and negotiate with Michael Gecan of the Metro Industrial Areas Foundation (IAF), who, in the tradition of many of the best organizers, kept his name off TV but made it painfully familiar to those in power by forcing a living-wage bill through the New York City Council and making it stick despite Giuliani's veto.[3]

When Sarah Palin scoffed at Barack Obama's qualifications for the presidency by telling the 2008 Republican National Convention, "I guess a small-town mayor is sort of like a 'community organizer,' except that you have actual responsibilities," she may not have understood what she was saying but she had hit on part of the idea. An organizer doesn't have an actual set of responsibilities save that of putting the responsibility of self-determination where it belongs, on the people themselves.

Saul's understanding of the community organizing business was almost as nebulous as Palin's. For Saul organizing varied in method, shape and scope depending on the times and the circumstances. Sometimes he talked about organizing through the committees of correspondence leading up to the Revolutionary War and sometimes he speculated about how one might have organized an underground resistance to the Nazis in Germany. It was not organizing communities that Saul was about but organizing people.

Had it not been for the Great Depression he might have made archaeology his calling, but that unexpected fellowship brought him to criminology and hanging out with gangsters. His association with Frank ("the Enforcer") Nitti (circa 1888–1943), a major figure in Al Capone's organization or "public utility," as Saul used to refer to it, introduced Saul to the application of various forms of power.

One of his favorite Nitti stories concerned the gangster's meeting with Anton Cermak (1873–1933) shortly after Cermak was elected mayor of Chicago in 1931. Nitti had requested the meeting to negotiate the amount of money the Capone organization would have to pay to continue to provide the city's speakeasies with beer and other alcoholic products. As Saul told the story, Cermak explained to Nitti, "You know I was elected as a reform candidate." To which Nitti replied, "What the hell does that mean, Tony?" and waited for an answer. "It means," the mayor said after a suitable pause, "that the price is double."

While gangsters did sometimes use sawed-off shotguns instead of lawyers to resolve contract disputes, the deeper Saul got into gangland, the less interesting it became. He found that the Capone organization had many of the trappings of a modern corporation. He recalled rooms at the boss's headquarters at the Lexington Hotel filled with men wearing green eye shades and starched collars at desks with hand-cranked adding machines making entries into ledgers. The crime syndicate, like every other business, kept track of profit and loss.

While still in his twenties, Saul became a criminologist at Illinois' major penitentiary at Joliet. Part of his job was to assess who was and who wasn't a good parole risk, a task he viewed with bleak fatalism. One day Saul read me a letter he had just received from Nathan Leopold. Leopold and his lover, Richard Loeb, two wealthy young men in their late teens, had been sentenced to life in prison for the murder of another young man. The crime and the trial had been one of the big mass media events of the 1920s.

Saul had known Leopold at Joliet and regarded him as a model prisoner. That may have been why the murderer wrote to ask the former penitentiary criminologist to support his petition for parole. Saul read me what he had written in reply. He told Leopold that he did indeed have an excellent record in the big house but went on to say that he had no idea why Leopold had killed his victim and therefore no way of guessing if he would do it again. Saul would not recommend Leopold's release.

The work at Joliet bored the easily bored Alinsky but he did have fun with the con men and one of the flimflam men initiated Alinsky into the secrets of his trade. In the course of his instruction he dared Saul to do him a favor and get him a dozen guinea pigs. Guinea pigs were as much contraband as opium and the institution was sealed as tight as a vacuum jar, with staff being searched as they entered and when they left. Saul could think of no way of sneaking the animals in.

At length he put the guinea pigs in a wire cage that he loosely covered in newspapers, drove down to Joliet to begin the day's work, presented himself for the routine search holding the cage with the defecating, dripping animals who were scurrying around under the newspaper and was waved in without so much as an inquiring murmur.

Some weeks later Saul recounted that he was standing in the prison yard with the warden, who, he said, was a tough hombre, when whisk! A guinea pig ran by. A few minutes later another one ran in front of the warden and then another. There followed a conversation more or less to this effect:

"A lot of guinea pigs around here lately, Warden."

"Yea."

"We could trap 'em and get 'em out of here."

"Like hell. What's outta here stays outta here an' what's in here stays in here. No exceptions."

It was not all skittles and beer at Joliet. Saul made enemies, one of whom was a gangster named Roger Touhy (1898–1959). In exchange for a bribe he wanted Alinsky to arrange favors for him. When Touhy was refused he said that he would even the score one day. This didn't bother Saul since Touhy was serving a ninety-nine-year sentence, but in 1959 a federal judge granted the convict a writ of habeas corpus. When Saul heard about it he told me to be ready to throw the family in a car and camp out in a motel in Michigan or Indiana at least a hundred miles away from Chicago. It did not come to that. One evening as Touhy was going up the front stairs of his sister's house two men with shotguns ended his life.

Whether Touhy actually was a problem after so many years was doubtful. His northwest-side gang had decomposed by the time he was sprung and I don't think Saul thought that there was much danger. He explained to me that in situations such as this you make sure the other party understands that, even if you or your kith and kin are killed, arrangements have been made to reciprocate. If Saul called up some of his old friends and asked them to provide reciprocity he did not tell me.

Saul's time at Joliet convinced him that the odds on successful rehabilitation programs were not promising. He came to believe that by the time most of the men were driven in shackles through the penitentiary's gates they were irremediably set in who they were and only advancing years would lessen their chances of becoming repeat offenders. He was not much more sanguine about most of the programs aimed at teenage gangs, seeing little connection between such things as athletic programs and the lessening of juvenile delinquency. As Saul would say, the baseball bat used to hit a home run was also handy for cracking open someone's noggin. He looked on adolescent males as "nature's natural fascists."

During the course of organizing in a Chicago south-side African American neighborhood one of our people, a man with a genius for bringing people together and then not knowing what to do next, organized a group of boys and young men who hung around East Sixty-second Street and South Blackstone Avenue. Putting together this seemingly harmless group contravened Alinsky's oft-repeated injunction against organizing teenage males. You don't do it, Saul would say, for the same reason that you do not give little boys machine guns. When I found out that this group of little boys had been handed machine guns, I ran to Saul for advice as to what to do.

His answer was keep them busy twenty-four hours a day, never let up, keep them dogtrotting in close formation, never be without a project for them or they will think one up for themselves. At no small cost in energy our anti–idle hands program kept the devil and his work at bay. The Blackstone Rangers were a help doing such things as acting as marshals at demonstrations but in time new staff came, old staff left, the supervision broke down. The organization commenced changing its name and with each new moniker it grew more dangerous. From the Blackstone Rangers it transmogrified into, among others, the Black P. Stone Rangers, the Almighty Black P. Stone Nation and the El Rukn Tribe of the Moorish Science Temple in America. Please do not hold me to these names with exactitude but what was a sure thing is that they got guns, and the murders and mayhem began. When Martin Luther King came to Chicago in 1966 for his ill-fated campaign, the Rangers, after being recruited by a witless King assistant, made their contribution by engaging in a short, snappy gun battle with the East Side Disciples in a YMCA shortly before King was to appear to make a speech.[4]

Still, Saul died just as the tidal wave of drug convicts was beginning to flow into the nation's prisons, bringing with it a somewhat different population, many thousands of whom were nonviolent drug offenders. He might have modified his opinion on the hopelessness of rehabbing a higher percentage of these convicts, for if there ever was a person not wedded to doctrine or dogma and open to changing his opinion when the facts changed it was he.

As Saul studied gangs and juvenile delinquency he said he came to believe that the social setting the kids were born into would have to be changed. As long as children were inescapably destined to grow up in an environment in which they had to join in gang life to protect themselves, programs premised on individual redemption could have only limited success. Saul was looking for what today is called a holistic approach, though I doubt he would use that kind of vocabulary.

In 1939 Saul's antidelinquency project sent him into Chicago's Back of the Yards neighborhood. The yards in question were the city's slaughterhouses and meatpacking plants, Carl Sandburg's "Hog Butcher for the World," where millions of cattle, hogs and sheep were slaughtered, butchered, packed and dispatched by refrigerated railroad cars to the nation's dinner tables.

In back of the meatpacking plants the workers lived in perfect disharmony, heavily Polish in composition but with seven or eight other ethnic groups in permanent struggle within themselves and with each other. In its poverty, low wages, unemployment, dilapidated housing, dirt and strife the Back of the Yards was prototypical of late-nineteenth- and early-twentieth-century industrialism run amok in the heedless conduct of its business.

A permanent stink hung in the air, ranging day to day in quality from disgusting to revolting. Most of the thousands of packinghouse workers lived on sliver-thin lots in creaky, wooden houses that looked as though they might tip over, being twice as high as they were wide. The ground floor was often seven or eight feet below street level, flooding during heavy rains. And at the very back of these narrow lots would be an outhouse and yet another dwelling.

The men and women who trooped out of these dearly bought and precariously held homes to work their shifts in the packinghouses were of Polish (the largest group), Bohemian, Slovak, German, Irish and Mexican extraction. Many spoke English with difficulty if at all, and none of them spoke to each other. Each nationality had its own parish, parochial school and convent. Services were conducted in each group's language and nobody, clergy included, had anything to do with the other.

Saul recognized that if every Lithuanian boy was forced to join a gang to fight off every Polish or Irish or Mexican kid, who also was forced to join a gang to protect himself, the violence and futility would never be broken. But the predicate for peace was unity and from the 1880s onward attempts to organize a union were defeated by the meatpackers' management, who played ethnic and racial groups against each other. Unity would have to be forged out of this body of hateful animosities.

Saul had other goals. He hoped that in bringing unity to the Back of the Yards, its people would come to play a part in the mobilization of the region and the nation in the battle against fascism. That preyed on Alinsky's mind because Hitler looked to be much more dangerous in 1939 when it seemed he might duplicate the conquests of Napoleon than he does in the stale newsreels on the History Channel whose viewers watch with knowledge of who won.

An organizer who goes to a place at the invitation of some kind of local committee has a few people who will answer questions frankly and help as much as they can. Saul did not have that when he began nosing around the Back of the Yards. He was on his own as he began the laborious process of convincing people he was not a cop, a bill collector, a repo man, a con man, a white slaver or a subversive. The story of how the Back of the Yards Neighborhood Council (BYNC) was organized is best told elsewhere in Alinsky's own words. (See *Reveille for Radicals* and also *Back of the Yards: The Making of a Local Democracy* by Robert A. Slayton.) As the council came into existence so too did the idea and definition of a community organization, at least as the term is used today. In its current definition I doubt that Alinsky would have much use for it in the changed society we live in. The least doctrinaire of men, he would in all likelihood be tinkering with new ways to realize the old goal of democratic self-rule.

As the BYNC came together Saul realized that community organization was, among other things, a powerful tool for winning strikes or battles with the rich, the politically privileged and the entrenched of all sorts. "There is the management," Saul would say, "sitting at its desk. On the desk there is a row of buttons. One says police, another says church, another says newspapers, another courts, another local politicians, another says TV stations, another banks and credit unions, clubs, the National Guard, Little League and the schools and social work agencies. When a strike is threatened the guy at the desk begins pushing the buttons and one by one all these organizations and institutions are mobilized against the strike or whatever situation is at issue and you are smashed.

"What community organization does is it comes along with a pair of scissors and one after another it quietly snips the wires attached to the buttons. When the guy hits the buttons, nothing happens and the battle is won."

The corollary is that even if all the workers in a company are organized and determined to hold out until the end of time or if all the members of a community or any other group are united and dedicated to the cause but they lack outside support and backup, the odds are you will lose. In some situations where it was impossible to snip all the wires, Saul would try to win over public opinion. If that wasn't likely he would say, "We're not going to try it."

Saul is remembered as a superbly imaginative tactician, the Great Wiggler able to come up with an idea that disorganized the other side in the most adverse situations. Yet Alinsky, the man with the reputation for combative truculence, knew when not to fight. Part of his genius was the ability to recognize an unwinnable situation.

He had learned from watching John L. Lewis, the dominant figure in organized labor's ascent to mass membership in the 1930s. Lewis was able to win apparently unwinnable strikes. He did it, however, with the resourceful derring-do that only leaders at the pinnacle of the talent pyramid possess.

Saul loved to tell the story of Lewis at his grandest during the 1936–37 organizational strike at General Motors. The workers at the Chevrolet plants in Flint, Michigan, had sat down inside the factories and announced that they were not leaving until they had a union contract.

General Motors had the police attempt to clear the plants, but they were met by employees hurling every metal object they could put their hands on. The police resorted to tear gas, but the workers' wives rushed up to the sides of the building and smashed the windows to allow the gas to escape.

The company went to court and got an order requiring Governor Frank Murphy of Michigan to use the National Guard to dislodge the disobedient workers. The order was quashed when it was learned that the judge was a major General Motors stockholder.

Lewis, who had his headquarters in Washington, took a night train to Detroit, where another judge was issuing another order and the National Guard was preparing for action. American management-labor relations seemed about to repeat the blood-lettings of twenty-three years earlier when twenty workers and family members of Lewis's own United Mine Workers were killed by members of the National Guard at Ludlow, Colorado.

Saul said that Lewis told him that well after midnight, with the Guard due to attack in the morning, there was a knock on his hotel room door. Standing there was Frank Murphy, governor of Michigan and future associate Justice of the United States Supreme Court, who told Lewis he could not sleep, thinking of the lives that surely would be lost in the morning. He begged Lewis to back off. Why should he? Lewis asked. Why was Murphy sending in the Guard?

Because it was the law.

Lewis reminded Murphy that the governor's father had been jailed by the British for breaking the law in the cause of Irish freedom and that Murphy's grandfather had been hanged by the same people for breaking the same law for the same reasons.

A shaken Murphy asked Lewis what he was going to do.

"Tomorrow morning I shall personally enter General Motors plant Chevrolet No 4. I shall order the men to disregard your order, to stand fast," Saul quotes Lewis as answering Murphy. "I shall then walk up to the largest window in the plant, open it, divest myself of my outer raiment, remove my shirt and bare my bosom. Then when you order your troops to fire, mine will be the first breast that those bullets will strike."[5]

The National Guard never came.

Saul loved that story; he loved the Lewisian bombast, the iron-jawed, indomitable hero, the victory of people who had never won before, the smoke and poetry of it. He prized it for its rarity, knowing how few such moments are.

But he didn't suggest imitating it. Most people, Saul used to say, had best learn when to fold 'em. The price paid by those who follow leaders who lack self-knowledge, whose anger or egos drive them into picking or prolonging the wrong fight, is defeat.

For Saul defeat was not a learning experience. It was a disaster. He understood that there are times when defeat is your inescapable portion, the wipeout of the Jews in the Warsaw Ghetto, for example, but he had no tolerance for a defeat that could have been avoided, no patience with moral victories. He had witnessed the way Communists sacrificed the interests of local people—union members or African American civil rights workers—to manufacture martyrs for the larger cause and he had no use for such exploitation of the innocent. He believed that an organizer's first responsibility is to the people he has recruited. They joined for better housing or justice or jobs or community self-determination, not to be used in behalf of a grander cause.

He understood why Martin Luther King conducted his campaigns for the larger goals of national legislation, even though after King moved on to the next town he may have left the local people broke, in jail, naked to retaliation and vulnerable to firings and harassments. The moral victory, the public relations tri-umph belonged to King and the movement, which was advanced accordingly, but Saul was aware of how the locals may have paid dearly for such progress, joining, as one internal civil rights movement memo put it, "a string of embittered cities."[6]

John L. Lewis and Alinsky organized adults, people who had families, children, jobs, mortgages, doctor bills, all the respon-sibilities of being grown-ups. For an adult with responsibilities the loss of a paycheck is often a family catastrophe. Saul was not big on provoking arrests.

He used to say if you are going to get your people arrested, you'd better make goddamn sure you've got the bail money and the lawyers to get 'em out of jail. That was not something that leaders in the anti–Vietnam War and civil rights movements would necessarily worry about, since most of the rank-and-file demonstrators in these movements were young, unmarried people, high school and college students, sometimes grammar school kids. Saul felt that while the getting-arrested tactic might be workable using teenagers, college students and that part of the clergy that has time on its hands for this modified form of martyrdom, with labor unions and other organizations whose membership is made up of adults with family responsibilities, arrests can wreck morale and be financially costly to organiza-tions whose treasuries are in precarious-enough shape without having to pay court fines.

As for staff getting arrested, Saul had an absolute prohibition. He would explain that a staff person cannot operate behind bars; besides the publicity that would come with the arrest belongs to the local people.

The 1963 March on Washington and the Selma march two years later were composed mostly of adults; the marchers came from everywhere across the nation, often sent by major organizations with, compared to demonstrators in other situations, little at risk. Even taking into account the murder of Viola Liuzzo during the Selma march, these historically important events were relatively safe and protected occasions.

From Tiananmen Square to Teheran it is the young people out on the streets taking their chances and running the risks while in America at least antiwar demonstrations tended to be vacation time, warm-weather activities. That does not make their objectives less serious but implies different tactics than those an Alinsky or a Lewis would use.

Some criticize Alinsky's position on winnability. Urban historian Beryl Satter sees two "major flaws in Alinsky's model of organizing":

> his insistence that organizing efforts be fully funded before they could be launched, which left him vulnerable to pressure by wealthy donors, and perhaps more serious, his belief that they should tackle only issues that were "winnable."
>
> This stance was in stark contrast to the attitudes of the African American activists in Mississippi, who in the early 1960s were risking their lives for a goal that seemed impossibly utopian: the end of a reign of white supremacy that had been in place for generations. That same fearless attitude was needed in Chicago, where community groups in changing and black neighborhoods faced wealthy and entrenched opponents who were highly adept at evading moral, legal and economic

pressure. Unfortunately, Alinsky's insistence in fighting only for winnable ends guaranteed that his organizations would never truly confront the powerful forces devastating racially changing and black neighborhoods.[7]

These are intelligent and fair observations but mistaken insofar as Saul put winnability over risk taking. In the 1950s he went into the white southwest side of Chicago (Organization of the Southwest Community or OSC), a pot boiling over with racial hostilities. So far as I know the organizational drive there was the first and only attempt by anyone to organize nonliberal, nonuniversity middle- and lower-class whites.

Both the odds and omens were against success but he had a well-considered approach that he believed stood a good chance of realizing its goals. The right preparation could reduce the odds. What he would have no truck with was the kamikaze idealism of projects that he knew would fail. There were too few organizers and not enough money to take on ventures which had little to offer save good intentions. If a cause is worth fighting for, Saul would repeat, you have a responsibility to prevail. The work is too important for sentimentality. It demands that you pick your shots. Not all injustices can be righted.

Saul did not believe in lost causes. If someone wanted his help on a project doomed to fail, he would slough it off, as Sidney Lens, a valiant, if somewhat knuckleheaded, lefty, found out back in the late 1930s when the Back of the Yards Neighborhood Council was being organized.

Lens had gotten a job in Meyer Bros. Department Store in the neighborhood but was canned when management found out that he was trying to sign people up for membership in the Department Store Employees Union Local 291. Local 291 was more a bundle of dreams than a functioning labor union, but, as he later wrote, to aid its cause Lens set up a one-man picket line outside the store, with occasional relief from members of the Packinghouse Workers Union. "The only hope of getting my job back was to institute a boycott and, since there was a strong Back of the Yards Council in the neighborhood headed by Saul Alinsky . . . that seemed a promising channel." But when Lens met with Alinsky and neighborhood priests, he was "surprised to find them unsympathetic. Alinsky . . . was acerbic. At any rate, I was not helped by the council and without it a boycott was doomed."

When writing about it years later, Lens implied that the failure of the BYNC to back his boycott might have been due to the fact that Meyer Bros. carried a two-page ad in the council's newspaper. Knowing Saul, it is reasonable to suppose that the ad and, more important, the support of local merchants in general played a part in denying Lens assistance, but organizing of this kind is so precarious you cannot be distracted by every act of injustice which may come stumbling at you. You have to keep focus. You do not have the energy or resources to allow yourself to get distracted by the world of good and noble causes out there. If you do and you keep bringing up injustices done to one-man bands like Lens, you will confuse and exhaust your membership and when that happens everything else unravels.[8]

One of the reasons that Saul had a certain contempt for liberals or progressives and called himself a "radical" was that he suspected liberals of being losers. He shared with conservatives the feeling that liberals were soft, that they would buckle in a crisis and quit the field. He did not trust them or believe that they could be counted on in a fight.

For him a radical was not a devotee of an ideology. For him a radical was someone who was mentally tough, who could keep his fears to himself, who did not panic, who did not dither, who did not use the finer points of morality to evade action, who did not come down with the blues or misgivings or a sudden need to split hairs and think up reasons for delay.

Alinsky was aware of the perils Beryl Satter describes. Yes, you could be "vulnerable to pressure by wealthy donors," which is why Alinsky banked the money for an organizational drive before he started it. Once you gave to the Industrial Areas Foundation you did not get it back. Money was hard to come by from sources willing to back what Alinsky wanted to do. For years the IAF machine was little more than paper clips and rubber bands. Pay was meager. There was no health insurance and certainly no retirement program. Such would come years later after Alinsky's death when the IAF was no longer as controversial an operation.

Saul detested money raising. In the early years of the IAF the chances of getting a foundation grant awarded to a one-man operation when the one man had a reputation as a bomb thrower were remote. There were few sources of funds but the very rich. The very liberal very rich, that is, of whom there were a limited and sometimes quirky supply.

Some of the board members on whom he depended for the IAF's slim budget were the kind of knowledgeable, involved people who did not have to have Saul entertain them in order to open their purses. For others, it helped when he acted as though he'd just come in off the mean streets, a tough, film-noir sort of guy. He was expected to have a certain amount of dirt under his fingernails to prove his authenticity.

When in the mood or when the occasion called for it, he could take on some of the mannerisms of an unpolished guy from Factoryland to coax contributions. The donors appreciated hearing the latest dispatches from the battlefront where class warfare was being waged and he loved telling his stories and was good at it.

His experiences raising money for the IAF provided Saul with a collection of odd-man-out stories in which he played the unhip dumb bunny from the lower orders. One was about a formal five-course dinner at the Park Avenue home of Adele Rosenwald Levy, one of the Sears, Roebuck heirs. The fish was delicious and every time the server offered more, Saul helped himself. Every time he helped himself, the server offered more. Finally, stuffed to the gills, he was offered the next course. Too full to partake of it, Saul always claimed that he had lodged a complaint with his hostess. He should have been told that roast beef was coming.

These one-sided relationships with the rich were a burden and an irritant. You never knew what they might do next. On one occasion Saul and Levy were walking in Manhattan when they stopped in front of Abercrombie & Fitch, not the store currently bearing the name but the old one that had supplied the guns and ammunition for Teddy Roosevelt's expeditions. She told Saul to pick out for his own any one of the items displayed in the window. With a small shrug of the shoulders, he said to himself,

"What the hell?" and pointed at a leather armchair. In due course it made its appearance in Chicago.

Saul was always envious of his friend Myles Horton (1905–1990), the founder of the Highlander Folk School in Tennessee, where Pete Seeger made the final changes on "We Shall Overcome" and Rosa Parks was prepped for her bus ride into history. Myles had a mellifluous mountain accent that he had held onto despite studies at the University of Chicago and the Union Theological Seminary. In soliciting funds from northern liberals, Myles was also aware of the donors' desire for "authenticity" and Saul noted that "the closer Myles gets to New York, the heavier his accent." Saul could not do accents, not even his mother's pronounced Yiddish and when he'd try, I'd cringe. All Saul had to prove his authenticity were his stories of the poor and occasionally growly wisecracks spoken out of the side of his mouth.

THREE

CARRYING THE BIBLE ACROSS THE COLOR LINE; FIVE REA-
SONS ALINSKY DIDN'T ORGANIZE IN THE SOUTH IN THE
1950s; RACE WARFARE; WORKING WITH THE COMMUNISTS;
ALINSKY AGAINST THE SEGREGATIONIST MAJORITY IN THE
BACK OF THE YARDS; "SOME ONE ELSE OUGHT TO COME
AND ORGANIZE AGAINST ME"

O ne of the unwinnable fights Saul did not take on was an organizing campaign in the South. In the 1950s Alinsky and I
talked about it a lot.

My own experience in the South had come after finishing at
a Jesuit high school in the Bronx. I'd gone to Chicago to attend
college, but I did not do well in schools. I wanted to be shut of
sitting on wooden seats in classrooms, so once I'd arrived in
Chicago, I spit the bit and skipped college. I had no plan. I tried
to support myself through a series of jobs, the most arduous of
which was working behind a "gut buggy" in a meatpacking plant
where I was a member of the union Saul had helped to organize,
though I knew nothing about that at the time.

The men I met in the packinghouse whetted an interest in learning about the people who lived on the other side of the wall that separated the black and white races in Chicago. I began visiting the holiness churches on south State Street, where black working-class people worshiped.

A couple of graduate students in sociology took an interest in me and scrounged up a little money to enable me to go south and meet the holiness people in rural Mississippi, Alabama and Tennessee. This was before *Brown v. Board of Education*, when, except for he-ing and she-ing in the dark out of the moonlight, no interracial contact on an equality basis was allowed. The only exceptions who were permitted to circulate in the black community without danger of tar and feathering were ministers and possibly medical personnel.

I took to carrying a large Bible and the white people drew their own conclusions. I told the black people that I was a student come to learn how things were with them. They took me at my word, although two or three times I was invited to speak to the congregation. In Memphis I was invited by some of the younger church people to several long bull sessions. It was the first eye-level conversation they had had with somebody of the other race. Once they felt comfortable they told me what they really thought and felt. It would be the younger brothers and sisters and children of these men and women who would do the sit-ins and marches ten or fifteen years later.

More than one black farm family invited me to stay with them. It was generous and risky for a family to take in a white stranger who had nothing to offer them but an ear and a lot of questions.

In Holmes County, Mississippi, the family I stayed with had no well and therefore no water. Instead they had a wagon on top of which was an extra-large wooden barrel. With the wagon hitched up to the mule, they fetched their water from a source several miles away. The second night I spent with them, I woke up around three o'clock and inched myself out of bed, trying not to wake up the two sons of the family on either side of me. I snuck out to the front yard and looked up at the stars. It was a clear night in which there were so many it seemed as though somebody had overdone it. I stared at them and asked myself, "Are you crazy?"

After leaving the South I spent a brief interlude in Boston, where I worked for Joe Cass, then political director of the state CIO, as an apprentice political flunky. With Joe it was politics at the street level, trying to get city councilmen or state representatives elected. I spent a lot of time with bookies, welfare mothers, business agents of creaky old union locals, third-tier gangsters and candidates who knew less about politics than I did. Joe gave lessons on how to navigate the mean streets and keep one's ideals intact and Joe, like Saul, did not think I was crazy.

After long discussions about organizing in the South, Saul decided against it. It was not attempted for five reasons.

The first reason. Any southern move, Alinsky believed, would almost immediately result in the IAF's tax exemption being lifted. Without the exemption the IAF was out of business. He discussed protecting the exemption with Senator J. William Fulbright, a Democrat from Arkansas, a major figure among Dixie Doges, the southern clique which ran Congress in that era, but a clandestine liberal. Make that a very clandestine liberal. Fulbright's opinion in which Saul concurred was that there would be a wholesale attack against us as Communists which would make the lifting of the exemption impossible to stop. Such money as we were operating on was mainly from religious sources and one small gutsy foundation that would not legally be able to give to an organization with a canceled tax exemption.

The second reason. We did not know who we might be able to organize. Even though the Montgomery bus boycott that Dr. King headed—although he did not organize it—was an adult operation, we thought that organizing African American adults in the South would be extremely tough. The NAACP had chapters in large towns and small throughout the region whose members were adults, but for the most part they were not out demonstrating but were inside raising money and providing other kinds of support for civil rights litigation.

Even so their people were in danger of retaliation. Later on in the 1960s the young people in the Student Nonviolent Coordinating Committee (SNCC) who conducted sit-ins and what to white eyes were brazen acts of defiance railed at the NAACP for its caution, but they did not have children, aged parents, mortgages and white bosses.

While Dr. King may have preferred to have grown-ups in his line of march, he often had to rely on heroic youngsters.

The third reason. We thought that the South was the wrong place. It seemed that the most important changes in civil rights and race relations would take place in the South with its history of slavery, Jim Crow laws and Dixie's flamboyant place in the national folklore, but in those years it was still an economic and industrial backwater. The decision-making centers of America were in the cities of the North and West.

Moreover, although Chicago had an African American congressman and other elected officials, it was, if you examined the census, more segregated than Mississippi, Alabama, Georgia or any other state in the Old Confederacy. Blacks and whites shared washrooms and sat together in the downtown movie theaters, but outside of downtown an African American stood about the same chance of being served in a restaurant in Chicago as he would have in Jackson, Mississippi.

The whites of Chicago entertained racial myths every bit as screwy as those in the Deep South. Many white Chicagoans in that period believed that the NAACP periodically designated certain days as "shove days" when blacks on buses, in subways and on the sidewalks were supposed to shove or push or bump any white they happened to be close to. Hundreds of taverns in the white areas of the city's south and west sides could be entered only after the barkeep got a good look at your face and then hit a buzzer, releasing the door lock.

Two African American friends and I unknowingly walked into the Wharf, a "white" tavern on the corner of Fifty-fifth Street and Stoney Island Avenue via an unwatched side door, were refused service and were confronted with a small mob of thirty or so people. It wasn't only the men. Women in the crowd had taken off shoes and were ready to go after us with their stiletto heels. We barely escaped alive.

Throughout most of the 1950s, with police connivance, what amounted to a minor race war fitfully raged around the Trumbull Park Homes, a public housing project on the far southeast side. The newspapers and radio and TV stations had acceded to an unofficial agreement not to publish or broadcast news of interracial violence without the concurrence of city hall. There were, as far I know, no African Americans on the staffs of major Chicago media with the exception of the black-owned and -read *Chicago Defender*. When I left Saul in 1963 to work for the *Chicago Daily News*, the night city editor had the habit of introducing me to visitors as "our niggerologist."

A white Chicagoan remembered being taken to a wedding reception by a friend in a south-side working-class neighborhood:

> Guys started getting up, getting their coats and leaving, saying "Let's go," and my friend's older brother came over and told us what was going on: we were all expected to join in. There had been some kind of crime committed against a white person by a black—I don't recall what it was. They were all getting in their cars and getting guns and railroad flares, and they were driving to the nearest black neighborhood, and they were going to shoot up houses and throw flares through windows, things like that. These were not people who fucked around. . . . And you had that all over the white South Side. You're not dealing with a bunch of pantywaists from the suburbs. These are hard people.[1]

The white part of Chicago was a honeycomb of conspiracies to confine black people to "their" part of the city. The banks, savings and loan institutions, government, churches, schools, hospitals, fire and police departments, news media, the Real Estate Board—everybody was part of it. No institution, low or high status, refrained from keeping the burgeoning black population penned up in sections exploding with people. The University of Chicago belonged to a neighborhood group that bought up vacant houses it feared might be purchased by an African American family. The following bit of doggerel in the handwriting of the university's president Robert M. Hutchins reflects the same upper-class determination to keep blacks out as that of neighborhood leaders in white working-class areas:

> The Chancellor and the President gazed out across the park.
>
> They laughed like anything to see that things were looking dark.
>
> "Our neighborhood," the Chancellor said, "once blossomed like the lily.
>
> "Just seven coons with seven kids could knock our program silly."
>
> "Forget it," said the President, "and thank the Lord for Willie."
>
> (Who Willie was and how he assisted the Lord in black exclusion is lost in time.)[2]

Similar combines existed everywhere in the city. African American families unlucky enough to buy a home in a white section ran the risk of going without fire, ambulance or police service just when they needed it most. How any adult white Chicagoan could go south to tell the people there how to order their affairs was a bit much in Saul's opinion.

Saul was also certain that northern cities were teetering on the edge of race warfare or something close to it. We would speculate about which northern city would blow its cork first. Saul was convinced that it would be Los Angeles with its renowned police chief Parker, who was given to calling African Americans monkeys. The L.A. police were so tightly wound in their crisp uniforms and shiny boots, behind their wraparound sunglasses, that they scared white people.

Alinsky was proven right when the City of Angels broke out in a mini civil insurrection in 1965. Much of the Watts area was torched as thirty-four people lost their lives and more than a thousand were wounded. The conflagration in Watts seemed to be the match which lit the Chinese firecracker of riots. The next five years they broke out in countless northern cities only to subside into the grim, heroin-filled 1970s and then to flare up in another form with the crack epidemic and its attendant street violence of the 1980s.

The fourth reason was that the two places Saul wanted to work in were New York City and Chicago, especially Chicago. He loved the city of his birth, and although in the 1950s its long decline had set in, it was not yet visible. It was still the imperial city of the Midwest, the center where America converged in dynamic, violent, creative turbulence.

The fifth reason was the Back of the Yards Neighborhood Council which had accomplished great things in the time between its founding at the end of the 1930s and the middle of the 1950s. What had been an area of ramshackle, near-slum housing tilting this way and that had been rebuilt into a model working-class community of neat bungalow homes. It had also become an impregnable fortification of whites-only exclusionism.

When Saul began his organizational work in the Back of the Yards it was worth a black man's life to walk down Ashland Avenue, the neighborhood's main drag. African Americans had been used as strikebreakers and union busters in times past and people remembered. They were not so quick to acknowledge the part that people from the Back of the Yards and nearby Irish Bridgeport played in the 1919 race riot during which thirty-seven people were killed and more than five hundred wounded, the majority of whom were African American. Spearheading the white attacks was Ragan's Colts, a political, social and athletic organization based in the area. The fighting did not end until the National Guard was thrown into the battle.

At the time of the organization of the BYNC a goodly contingent of African Americans worked in the packinghouses, so if the members of the two races were not able to work together at least on a limited basis the division between them would be exploited and the meatpackers would smash yet one more union and everybody else would lose.

One of the early successes of the council was the achievement of a degree of interracial cooperation which allowed the unmolested passage of black people through the Back of the Yards. In the present "postracial America" it may take an exercise of imagination to understand that there were many parts of northern cities where it was dangerous for African Americans, especially men, to traverse, but it was so and it may still be in many places. The council was also able to arrange the hiring of a few black clerks in the stores without their losing business.

This degree of amity was brought about through the white Catholic parishes, social clubs, merchants, ethnic associations and not a few of their black counterparts on the other side of the dividing line. They were able to convince and pressure would-be violent spirits. As important was working with the Packinghouse Workers Organizing Committee, the top man of which was Herb March, a card-carrying Communist, as they used to say. He was an accomplished organizer, an outstanding speaker and a man of such determination that even after an attempt was made to assassinate him as he was driving his car he never thought of packing it in and clearing out.

Saul thought highly of March and besides there was no choice but to work with him or kiss the idea of organizing packinghouses good-bye. Top-notch organizers—not social worker types, but hardened, cool organizers who can work effectively in high-pressure situations—are very, very rare. One of the things Saul used to say is that often critics think that in tight situations you have many more choices than you actually have. This was one where there was a wide spectrum of things you could think up to do, but it came down to working with the Communists or bagging it.

Sixteen years later in the 1950s the Communists had been squeezed out of the United Packinghouse Workers of America, which mattered little because the meatpackers themselves were closing their plants and moving out of town. The Back of the Yards community, however, was not one of those places where the major employer had gone elsewhere, leaving rack and ruin. The people had moved on to other, often better employment, and the community instead of being deserted was being revitalized by massive home remodeling and new construction, all being orchestrated by the BYNC.

The Back of the Yards Neighborhood Council, Alinsky's first community organization, was so successful in rebuilding and revitalizing the area that it became a stable rock of racial exclusion. Joseph Meegan, Saul's partner in organizing the council, went on to start an annual community fair which raised so much money through various forms of illegal gambling that the council achieved financial independence. It had no need of United Way money or foundation grants or government handouts, thus giving the opponents of racial exclusion no economic fulcrum to leverage the explosively difficult work of changing policies.

The council had become a model of how a white community can stay white. The motto was "We the people will determine our own destiny" and the people had decided their destiny was purely Caucasian. It pained Alinsky personally and at the same time not a few liberals regarded Saul as the progenitor of one of the most effective segregationist institutions this side of the Ku Klux Klan.

All would change for the better, or so Saul thought, if four or five carefully selected highly middle-class black families could be induced to buy homes in the Back of the Yards and their neighbors could be induced not to set fire to them. In hopes that something of the sort could be made to happen Saul went to see

Meegan who, after the council had been organized, had stayed on to run it with spectacular success. Joe was a serious Roman Catholic. His brother was a priest and secretary to Bernard J. Sheil, the Archdiocese of Chicago's powerful auxiliary bishop. Joe came from the neighborhood. Saul once said he was perfect for the work there because he was Irish and the one thing all the warring Slavs could agree on was their dislike of the Irish. Saul was kidding. Nobody disliked Joe Meegan, who was immensely popular in the community and in Mayor Richard J. Daley's city hall.

Though the backgrounds of the two men were so different, they were not only good friends but shared the same ideas about community and small-*d* democracy. Nonetheless, Saul's meeting at Joe's house to discuss the BYNC's lily-white problem ended in the two men shouting at each other. To Meegan even public discussion of a Negro family would have the same effect as news that the bubonic plague was loose in the community. Back of the Yards whites, who did not dislike black people, were united with most other home-owning whites in Chicago in believing that the first African Americans to move into the neighborhood were the harbingers of slumification, crime, bad schools and punishing drops in real estate values. At the time racial antipathies knew few bounds in a city which had as many derogatory words for black people as Americans have for genitalia or Eskimos have for snow.

As far as Joe Meegan was concerned the mere idea would cause an eruption which would destroy the community and the council, which had been his life's work. The two men never got to the practicalities, the first of which would be finding three or four African American families insane or brave enough to consider putting themselves and their children through the ordeal that would await them.

Intervention to thwart what is at least temporarily the will of a majority contradicted what Alinsky stood for but in the case of the Back of the Yards Council he was confronted with a democratic organization, one of his own creation, that had gone sour. It was 100 percent for racial exclusion. Saul could walk away from it, but he could not publicly attack it. That would have offended his code of loyalty. The leaders behind the whites-only policy were his friends, men and women he had gone to war with against the meatpackers and the Democratic Party political machine in the old days. In another connection Alinsky once told a newspaper reporter, "It just might be necessary for me to go back and organize against the organization I set up. And then, ideally, some one else ought to come and organize against me."[3]

Loyalty or not, I believe that Saul would have gone to war against the council if he had had an army, which he didn't. Making empty statements on the subject was no substitute for ending segregation in the Back of the Yards.

Saul, who retained the title of technical adviser to the council, was under pressure from liberal integrationists, who themselves lived in all-white communities, to denounce it and say that he was no longer connected with the organization. We would explain that we did not have the power to integrate the Back of the Yards, but one of the drawbacks of Saul's having the reputation of being a master Machiavelli was that it engendered the idea that we could do almost anything we wanted to do. (The plus of such a reputation is that you could scare the hell out of somebody by raising an eyebrow.)

Not that a public attack would have netted anything more than a two-day newspaper story. We would brainstorm about some other way to insert a knife to shuck that oyster but we could not come up with a feasible way to open up the area. With the BYNC we failed.

Saul used to ponder what he considered the contradictions inherent in his life's work. What is to be done when "the people" democratically decide to do something that you, the organizer, abhor? If there are any open-and-shut answers to that question Saul did not know them. He believed that in the long run the people would make the right decision.

FOUR

ORGANIZING BY BAMBOOZLE; STEALING VOTES FOR THE
OTHER SIDE; THE MINISTERS AND "THE LAST OF THE RED
HOT MAMAS"; JOYRIDING IN THE BATMOBILE WITH A GANG-
STER PRIEST; SAUL PURRS AND CLOSES THE DEAL; SAUL AD-
VOCATES A RACIAL QUOTA

Viewed from the twenty-first century, what we did to try to integrate other areas may seem indefensible, but you had to
have been there. In Chicago African Americans could vote, could
use the public libraries, beaches and swimming pools and schools.
But if these were not segregated by law, they were by practice and
custom. In Chicago everybody was equal, everybody enjoyed their
civil liberties, yet the place was almost like pre–Nelson Mandela
South Africa.

Saul's belief that in the long run people allowed to make their
own decisions will make the right choice did nothing for the
short run, which was a problem. In 1958 the only thing people
in those southwest side districts wanted to hear from an organizer was a better way to keep their communities uniracial. The

IAF organizers could not promise them that, but we could seem to without saying so and justify our manipulative misdirections because a strong, democratically governed community organization would be able to tamp down or suppress violence and promote slow, orderly neighborhood transitions from white to black with a minimum of economic loss or exploitation and a modicum of interracial friendship between those coming in and those leaving.

To a greater or lesser extent we succeeded in doing that. In the process a lot of people got handled, jobbed, bamboozled and conned. They thought that they had a democratic organization, and in a way they did and in a way they didn't.

There were hundreds of meetings, conventions attended by several thousand people, all the mechanisms of self-rule, but everything concerning race, including the admission of black groups to the organization, was steered by Saul's stealthy minions. In fact, the social justice skids were so well greased, staff had to work with—I don't know what to call them—the conservative or racial xenophobes or antiblack or potentially violent faction to ensure they were not shut out and left feeling unrepresented. To accomplish this end there was a small amount of judicious ballot-box stuffing, as I recall. It had to be done because we had to keep the antis in the organization. They validated the claim that the organization was truly representative of all groups and interests in the community, the source of power and credibility. We also had to have them inside the organization believing that it was their organization and not outside it perfecting their Molotov cocktail–chucking technique.

So there was the contradiction. We organized people to determine their own destinies except when we determined them. Alinsky had a bluntness about such things. He did not try to rationalize them or deny that sometimes the majority could be so tragically and immediately wrong you could not stand aside and let the lynching proceed. To his way of thinking a majority trying to deprive a minority of basic rights had to be opposed.

In *Rules for Radicals* Saul wrote, "The organizer . . . who is committed to a free and open society is in that commitment anchored to a complex of high values . . . freedom, equality, justice, peace, the right to dissent. . . . [T]hey include the values in our own Bill of Rights. If . . . a community organization voted to keep blacks out, and claimed justification by virtue of the 'democratic process,' then this violation of the value of equality would have converted democracy into a prostitute. Democracy is not an end; it is the best political means available toward the achievement of these values."[1]

Although I always hoped I would not be asked about my motives, on the racial frontier of white areas close to where African Americans lived the question was tossed at me all the time. Any outsider interested in anything having to do with race was either an overwrought Christian or a Communist.

I was quick to abjure both motives and claim an interest in maintaining real estate values, community health and solidarity by working to ensure that no neighborhood would be "artificially overrun" or "flooded by panic-peddling speculators." The idea was that if every white neighborhood took some Negroes, the correct name then, no neighborhood would have too many. It sounds racist today, but in that period I was working to convince invisible, politically powerful men that they should stop cutting off fire, ambulance and police services to the homes of black families who had moved into white sections.

Whenever I needed to convince someone important to sign on with an organization, I would arrange a meeting with Saul. He was the closer, the guy in the automobile dealership whom the salesperson brought in to cinch the deal, to get the customer to sign on the dotted line. He had a way of purring at people that vamped them into agreeable plasticity, an ability to make complicated and ambiguous situations simple to understand. He could also find common ground with the damnedest people under the damnedest circumstances.

One of his best signings was the Rev. Arthur Brazier, a man of integrity, intelligence and stem-winding oratorical gifts. It was 1961 and we had to have him in the organization we were putting together in a low-income, half-slum area of Chicago's African American south side. Besides putting every available moment into building up his church, Brazier was not a man to buy a pig in a poke, at least not from me. I needed Saul to purr at him.

I arranged a dinner with the Reverend Brazier and another African American clergyman, Ulysses Blakeley of First Presbyterian Church, at the Empire Room at the Palmer House Hotel, a classy place in those days. But it had a floor show which I had not bothered to check out. Saul and I arrived before the two ministers and Saul picked up the card on the table which informed diners they would have the pleasure of being entertained that

evening by Sophie Tucker, "The Last of the Red Hot Mamas." I
can't remember if Saul called me an idiot, a moron or just a jerk
but it was too late to switch to a more sedate venue or kneecap
Sophie in her dressing room.

In short order the ministers came, and Ms. Tucker opened her
revue wearing a costume which might pass for a cowgirl outfit
in a bordello. Her first song was a raunchy ditty entitled something like "Two-Gun Pistol Pete." I looked at the clergymen,
wondering if they were about to skedaddle lest they be seen by
a member of their congregations. Saul began to purr, Sophie
began to twirl her pistols, the clergymen began to smile. When
the music stopped and the Last of the Red Hot Mamas had dis-
charged her final lubricious projectile, Saul had made the sale.

Saul also bagged Msgr. Patrick J. Malloy, the pastor and reigning monarch of a parish with a membership of some five thousand families, a huge operation with two churches, a grammar
and a high school, a hospital and a football field, all of which institutions, as I recall, were hooked up so that they could use city
water without paying for it. The monsignor was something of
an alcoholic, a bankroller and friend of the mayor's from boyhood, a skirt chaser, a Cook County deputy sheriff with a badge
to prove it who carried a revolver under his cassock, or packed
heat as they said in the gangster movies about men whose careers of crime P. J. knew more about than a scriptwriter.

One fine morning Malloy put down his drink and took me to
see an Al Capone biopic starring Rod Steiger as Al. As we
watched, P. J. would lean over and correct the movie's factual
errors. I remember him telling me just before Dion O'Banion, a

north-side gangster, was rubbed out that "Deeny didn't have a brogue."

Pat had a routine for scaring the bejabbers out of visitors. It began with drinks in the rectory in the morning and then Malloy, who in his cassock looked like the Little King in the comic strip of his era, would jump up and say, "Let's go to the ball game." His guest would be led downstairs to the garage where Pat kept the Batmobile, a souped-up Buick which he drove out of its resting place truly like a bat out of hell. He would turn onto Wentworth Avenue, a one-way south thoroughfare, driving north, horn blaring, brakes squealing, spinning the steering wheel one way and another as his petrified passenger could do nothing but stare at his white knuckles. At Thirty-fifth Street Malloy would turn and head for Comiskey Park. There he would drive up on the sidewalk where the fans were lined up buying tickets, catch the eye of the police sergeant, toss him the car keys and shout, "Look after it, will ya, Joe!" and charge into the stadium to occupy a box next to Mayor Daley's.

A shaken Jack Egan, who made the mistake of an automobile sojourn with Malloy, said he did not know how he escaped alive. I told him that he was probably safer than he thought. I had it on fairly reliable authority that back in his youth Pat was supposed to have been the best wheelman in Chicago and that he was in demand by the city's best bank-heist artists.

In the 1950s Malloy, in addition to his ecclesiastic duties, served, unbeknownst to his religious superiors, as the gangland's arbitrator when disagreements developed between Chicago's criminal organizations. Regardless of that, we had to have him in the nascent community organization we were laboring to put together. He was a major power, politically, socially, with the cops, with the fire department, with organized crime and with financial institutions in some of which he had very large deposits. We had to have him but he could not stand African Americans. A black family moving into his parish would be like the barbarian Mongols breaching the Great Wall of China and P. J.'s response would be the same as the Chinese emperor's.

I had been able to get him to agree that there might be one acceptable black man in Chicago, Rep. William L. Dawson, who, when he was elected to the House of Representatives about fifteen years before we arrived on P. J.'s doorstep in the late 1950s, was the only African American in Congress. Dawson and his organization were also an indispensable component of the Daley machine, delivering much needed lopsided majorities to the mayor. For those accomplishments Dawson had the priest's respect but that was not enough to get him to sign on to a community organization which would, in the not-too-distant future, have to oversee the peaceful settling in of a black family in his parish.

I asked Saul to come out to the lavish rectory Malloy had built with his ill-gotten gangster gains to close the deal. Malloy and I had become buddies—we went to the movies together, we went to see the Chicago White Sox sitting in his box next to the mayor's, we lifted elbows together—but I was too junior to reel in this fish and plop him in a creel.

Saul arrived, Malloy got out the bourbon and Saul brought up the name of a mobster I had never heard of but whom both men

knew. Then they began finding penitentiaries full of mutual un-
derworld friends and nostalgia set in.

Saul began to purr and then in a quiet, warm but assured way
he turned the conversation with one of those this-is-how-it-is
openers. He began with real estate considerations, a topic which
experience had taught him was usually of prime importance to
members of the clergy. He said that it was only a matter of time
before a black family moved into the parish somewhere, that if
someone set fire to their house and burned them out it would
stampede white families into selling and moving away because
parents are not going to bring up their kids in a battle zone. That
would decimate the parish and crash real estate values. He went
on to tell Malloy, who wasn't saying a word, that if there was an
incident, he would be in trouble.

The blame would fall on him as the man who had the power
to control the area's police and firefighters. The mayor was not
going to back him. Times were changing. President Eisenhower
had sent the regular army into Little Rock, Arkansas, to ensure
a handful of black children got into a white high school. The
powers that be were not going to let the Communists use a racial
incident for propaganda. What cinched it, however, was Saul's
explaining that it would embarrass the cardinal, which, Saul did
not need to explain, Malloy could ill-afford; the previous cardinal had banished Malloy to Buenos Aires, where he had lived in
exile for years.

The message was delivered in Saul's most palsy-walsy purr, as
if they were both on the same side puzzling out a problem, working out a solution to a bad situation. It worked. P. J. signed on
the dotted line. Saul had read him right.

Alinsky was chary about using appeals to principles, faith, morals and higher values when enlisting others. In the conversation with Malloy they were not discussed, although after people had agreed to the deal it was often as not slathered over with moralistic explanations.

Alinsky won his reputation for cynicism by insisting that most of us are moved to action by self-interest first, moral principles second, if at all. The Alinsky aesthetic was repellent to those who claimed to be motivated by disinterested commitment to the welfare of others. Saul liked doing business with a Pat Malloy who made no bones about where his interest lay and spared us the sermons.

Signing up Malloy brought money and the use of his name in contacting others, but Saul would point out that signing up presidents, pastors or chairs of organizations was an empty exercise unless there was a follow-up—going inside those groups and recruiting the rank and file. An organization of organizations is worthless if it consists of the officers, pastors and top brass consorting with each other without the active participation of their members.

Saul was iffy on the desirable life span of his progeny. From Alinsky's point of view some organizations outlive their usefulness, some become so much part of a status quo they no longer are disposed to fight for the betterment of the people they were created to serve, some turn to genteel or not-so-genteel racketeering and some become the power vehicle for a leader gone sour or a corrupt clique.

Saul had seen all of these, which is why he did not view an organization that had its day of glory and then went to seed and vanished as a disappointment or failure. The organization to which Malloy signed on flourished for a few years, presided over the coming of black families into the communities on Chicago's southwest side in quiet, peace and dignity and then evaporated. It did not bring forth a new era of racial amity but for Saul progress was a new set of problems. The ideals of liberty and personal freedom were, in his opinion, the legacy one generation left to the next, but liberty itself had to be won and refashioned in new ways that fit new times.

In 1959 in the midst of our trying to defang the worst of the antiblack housing conspiracies, Saul gave a speech discussing how the multiplying African American population trapped in their circumscribed areas might find decent places to live without bringing on the social and economic consequences the fleeing white population feared. The speech, delivered as testimony before the United States Commission on Civil Rights, said out loud what we had been whispering to the white people in the "threatened" neighborhoods. Neighborhoods would continue to flip from white to black with home owners of both races taking a financial beating unless every neighborhood everywhere had a minimum number of minority residents. This would mean there would be no all-white communities for whites to flee to. For that there would have to be some kind of a "quota."

How could a Jew, a member of a group which had suffered from them, advocate quotas? Was he suggesting a black family's constitutional rights be suspended so that some kind of governmental body could assign them a neighborhood to further Alinsky's integration scheme?

No, he had nothing so governmental or legally coercive in mind. He was talking about using the same voluntary, extralegal, nonofficial social mechanisms which made Chicago an apartheid-like city to try quotas, explaining that "an unjust instrument in one case can serve justice in another."

My recollection as to why Saul gave the speech is foggy, even though I think I contributed a couple of paragraphs. Saul was irked at what he called blowing "the trumpet for moral reaffirmations" on the topic and he had hopes it might ignite something with Joe Meegan and the council. We were forever taking flak over the neighborhood's hermetically sealed borders which kept so much as the thought of a person of color moving in an impossibility.[2]

As soon as newspaper reports of the speech hit the streets, the hostile reactions began. The hubbub rolled into the white area of the city's southwest side where we were organizing. It took only a couple of days for the IAF to be kicked out. We were being thrown out of meetings and having doors slammed in our faces. Showing up in some parts of the district meant risking a beating. The connection between Saul and the IAF and the organization we had started had to be severed, after which I had to sneak around hoping that the fear-crazed whites wouldn't recognize me as connected with Alinsky, the guy planning to use the quota idea to bring unprintables into the area in order to flip it racially and make millions.

FIVE

DR. KING AND HIS ONE-TRICK PONY; KING AND ALINSKY
CONTRASTED; ALINSKY'S TIGHT SHIP; GANGBANGERS IN
SLUMDALE; LEAVE THE LUMPENS TO DICKENS; OUTSIDE
VOLUNTEERS NEED NOT APPLY; FIND OUT WHERE YOU'RE
GOING BEFORE YOU GO THERE

The way Saul operated contrasted with what Martin Luther King did when the great civil rights leader made his ill-starred decision to come north and fling himself into Chicago. Bayard Rustin, one of the savviest and most effective people in the movement, had warned King, telling him, "You don't know what Chicago is like. . . . You're going to be wiped out."[1]

King arrived in Chicago in 1966 with a set of pluses Alinsky would never have. The preacher from Atlanta enjoyed a worldwide reputation, respect running to reverence and even adoration, oratorical skill of the first order and the moral high ground, enabling him to shame, silence and even coerce those opposed to him. He had courage, decency and undeviating conviction. As the maximum leader of an epochal social movement Dr. King also had a record of historic accomplishment, of, it might seem, never losing.

It was, however, a record based on surfing the curl of the wave. When the wave has spent itself the surfer is left on the shore with water sucking the sand away beneath his toes as it recedes down the beach and out to sea. King came to Chicago oblivious of Alinsky's injunction to know where you are and start from there. King did not know where he was, mistaking Chicago, Illinois, for Birmingham, Alabama.

During the Chicago campaign, I chanced to run into Dr. King in a Memphis, Tennessee, hospital where James Meredith had been taken after having been shot at the start of his one-man March Against Fear. He pulled me aside for a short conversation about his Chicago endeavor. He did not say so but I had the impression he was worried about it.

I told him that I thought it could succeed if he was prepared for trench warfare, which would demand tight, tough organization to take on the Daley operation with its thousands of patronage jobs, assistant precinct captains, precinct captains, chiefs of precinct captains and ward committeemen. I added it could not be done in less than two years. He listened. I could not tell if he had heard it before or didn't believe it, or if it was so out of his previous experience he didn't appreciate how decisive these organizational advantages were. Then he said we ought to talk again, but it never happened.

King arrived in Chicago with a large staff, some of whom were very talented, some very not talented and some crazy as hoot owls, but all bickering with each other and climbing over each other so as to be closest to their leader. Saul's staff did not bicker.

It was not a stripped-down, battle-station-ready group which King brought to Chicago. Unprepared, he took on a political organization backed by both parties, big business, the White House, the newspapers and many thousands of African Americans who had been cut in on what may or may not have been their fair share of the boodle. Although the city was severely segregated, it was not an example of the absolutely right versus completely wrong conditions which King had been dealing with in Dixie. Chicago blacks had been voting for generations. There was a black congressman, black aldermen, thousands of black people with patronage jobs. One of King's own lawyers, a major stay and prop for him over the years and an African American, was also a slum owner.[2]

King had begun his campaign with a dramatic gesture, moving his own family into an apartment in a slum building in one of the poorest, most woebegone African American sections of the city. It was painted and patched up for him but it still was no bargain. King's entry quickly degenerated into what might have been taken as an ill-conceived publicity stunt. To prevail, the effort would have had to be under the command of a decisive, even hard-hearted, leader but whether it was out of kindness or weakness, Dr. King seemed unable to say no or you're fired. Alinsky had no such compunctions.

The organizations Alinsky started were democratic but the organization he ran was not. He was the boss. Saul would joke about the IAF's being a democratic organization in which he had one more vote than all the others combined.

You could argue with Saul. He enjoyed it. He had no use for yes-men and was, compared to most of us, impervious to flattery. Not that he did not like it. He loved it, but he had a warning device that let him know when it got too thick and gooey. He was not threatened by disputatious underlings.

One night he and I were up arguing until almost four in the morning about continuing a school strike. I was for it because the repercussions across the city would be enormous but he said we had carried the strike to the point where we would be hit by an injunction and a contempt-of-court order. The organization would be smashed. He had seen enough of that with John L. Lewis's defiance of court orders. Finally, he told me the way it was going to be. And that is the way it was.

Although Dr. King's organization, the Southern Christian Leadership Conference, raised huge amounts of money, there was no control over how it was spent and not a little of it was spent by some of King's subordinates living on the highest part of the hog, a situation which was sufficiently well known that some of King's supporters complained about it in private to him. It was one of those situations constantly teetering on becoming a public scandal.

In contrast, Alinsky operated under exacting rules. You could not put the price of an English muffin and a cup of coffee on an IAF expense account without documentation. Until just a couple of years before his death, he flew coach class. I had dinner with him one night after I had left the IAF and was disturbed to see how tired he looked and began yammering at him to start flying in the front section of the plane. He did not want to do it because much of the travel was to give lectures, with the fees being turned over to the IAF.

Money was husbanded to the point of parsimony and Alinsky's account books were always ready for inspection. Saul had seen too many people ruined and too many causes embarrassed by somebody reaching for the cookie jar. He used to wonder at politicians' weakness for free rides in private airplanes and the vulnerability of people who use their expense accounts to augment their salaries. We were a cheap organization, always telling the people with whom we worked, "If you want an office, raise the money for the rent. If you want a secretary in the office, raise the money for the salary." Our line to the people we were organizing was that as long as we are putting up the money, we get to make the final decisions. Raise your own money and show us the door.

Saul had few staff people but those he did have were first-class organizers. King had many people, none of whom had demonstrated an ability to convert the enthusiasm and potential of the civil rights movement into the stable, ongoing kinds of organizations which get things done inch by inch, year by year. The divergent backgrounds of the two men reveal some of the reasons King is revered today but Alinsky is more useful.

Divinity school, studying theology, the chaotic individualism of the Calvinist tradition, the you-go-your-way-and-I'll-go-mine polity of the Baptist Church, these elements put their stamp on Martin Luther King. Alinsky, to the contrary, had seen John L. Lewis convert the insurrectionary spirit of American industrial workers in the 1930s into stable, disciplined unions that brooked little freelancing by individuals but won unheard-of benefits for their members.

Before King had decided to come north and try his luck, Alinsky's analysis of the King operation foretold its failure outside the South and after his assassination its disappearance from the scene. In 1965 Alinsky told an interviewer:

> The Achilles' Heel of the civil-rights movement is the fact that it has not developed into a stable, disciplined, mass-based power organization. This needs to be said out loud. Many of the significant victories that have been won in civil rights were not the result of mass power strategy. They were caused by the impact of world political pressures, the incredibly stupid blunders of the status quo in the South and elsewhere and the supporting climate created particularly by the churches. Without the ministers, priests, rabbis, and nuns I wonder who would have been in the Selma march. The tragedy is that the gains that have been made have given many civil-rights spokesmen the illusion that they have the kind of organization and power they need. Self-deception like this is easy to understand. But the truth is that the civil-rights organizations have always been minuscule in actual size and power. Periodic mass euphoria around a charismatic leader is not an organization. It's just the initial stage of agitation.
>
> Belatedly many civil-rights leaders have been rudely awakened to this situation. It remains to be seen whether they have the skill, sensitivity, and above all the infinite patience they will need.[3]

Organizing is akin to stringing beads to make a necklace. It demands patience, persistence and some kind of design. King's campaign in Chicago was short on beads and bereft of design.

King went into Chicago at the invitation of a few small civil rights organizations. Having made the dramatic gesture of moving himself and his family into the slums, he intended to build some kind of a local base, although in arriving as he did, King all but obliterated any significant part for the local people. It may not have been what he meant to do but he turned them into supernumeraries in an opera entitled "King in Chicago."

For a Christian clergyman such a ministry to the poor was carrying out biblical instructions. For an agnostic organizer with a cool eye it was an ill-advised decision. Had Dr. King studied the comings and goings of Saint Paul with Alinsky's eye, he might have taken note that his religion's top organizer of all time left the poor to Jesus while he went after people with at least a little substance. The injunction to "sell whatsoever thou hast, and give to the poor" may truly be, as the apostle said, "treasure in heaven," but such attention to the least of these will be of scant help to an organizer in forming a power base (Luke 18:22).

Amid gang-violence crises and such from the outset King seemed to be writing a text about how not to organize. "I don't want to be a missionary in Chicago," he announced, "but an actual resident in a slum section so that we can deal first hand with the problems. We want to be in a section that typifies all the problems that we're seeking to solve in Chicago."[4]

The gangbangers, who dominated the area whose name on the map was Lawndale but was called Slumdale, had a different take on Dr. King's presence. In the words of one of them, "The civil rights organizations that came to Chicago were not working with the hard-core people anyway. They were supposed to have been for the grass root but the middle class was running them. They didn't know the people. The people who wouldn't mind being in a riot were never touched. They were still out there standing on the corners, laying in the alleys, and in the summertime sleeping in the park at night."[5]

The Nobel Peace Prize winner had his outsider volunteers pounding on the doors where the hard-core people lived. They wanted to recruit them but for what purpose other than the grand generalities was ill-defined. Explaining to people exactly why he and his outside friends had come among them was a recurring obstacle during Dr. King's Chicago sojourn. King and his outsiders were cut from a different cloth. Those outsiders were, as far as I could tell, a hodgepodge of young white idealists, college kids and summer soldiers, most of whom had no knowledge of the people they were supposed to recruit. In the South the youthful white idealists were useful civil rights cannon fodder; in Chicago they were dead weight. Instead of pestering lower-income black people with their good intentions, they might have made a contribution if they had stayed home and organized white people in Chicago and environs who were nine-tenths of the problem.

It was the antithesis of an Alinsky operation where outside volunteers were generally shooed away not only because they got in the way but also because they didn't have any skin in the game. Laudable as it is to volunteer to help other people wrestle with their problems, effective organizations are built with people who have a direct and personal interest in their success. The task is to help the people build their own organization. Ideally the outsider is the catalyst, the invisible element who starts the process and goes away, although in real life things do not go that smoothly.

The lumpen proletariat or the poorest of the poor are worthless for founding a functioning organization. Once a powerful and effective organization is up and running the membership may want to try to help the very poor, but you cannot start with them.

They suffer from what some call social pathologies, meaning their lives are a chaotic sequence of emergencies, terrible coincidences and unforeseen disasters. The lumpens are accident prone and emotionally unstable. Their lives are a chain of bad news— gas is cut off, electrical service terminated, the landlord is evicting them, a cousin is in jail, the baby has to be rushed to the emergency room, one of the kids sassed a social worker and the family is getting cut off, the reigning male came home and beat the hell out of the mother, Wilson stole the food money, Janice is pregnant, Mother missed her appointment with the vocational counselor because she was drunk. The very poor are unreliable, not the stuff of organizations which are composed of people bound together by keeping their commitments. Dostoyevsky or Dickens described the lying, stealing, drunkenness, cruelty, cheating and betrayal of existence at the bottom of the heap.

From the moment he arrived in Chicago, King was the focus of attention. He and his staff were primary in forming an agenda heavy on abstractions and light on specifics. The local people were not shut out, but, as in the King campaigns in the South, their role was more to be led than to lead. When King and his staff arranged a mass meeting, it was attended by people from all over, including the white suburbs, but, as such gatherings had been in the South, it was a rally, not the cap on a series of deliberative meetings.

There had been none of the long, careful inquiries which typified the best of the Alinsky organizing drives. As time dragged by the King operation took on the look of Napoleon before Moscow, a little army stranded inside a vast and hostile terrain.

With the door-to-door canvassing an inchoate muddle, King used his fame to carry out a coup de théâtre. In overalls and accompanied by his wife, Coretta, staff and a media tail he descended on a falling-down wreck of a slum building which was without heat and proclaimed that the Chicago Freedom Movement was putting it under "trusteeship" by virtue of "supralegal" moral authority. The rents owing to the landlord would be used to make repairs.

An Alinsky operation working on the principle of "You must know where you are before you try to go someplace else" would have first found out who owned the building and what the owner's circumstances were. The King people did no such thing and were embarrassed when it was discovered that the slum landlord was an invalid octogenarian who said he would give the building to anyone willing to take over the mortgage payments.

Andrew Young, an important member of King's staff, later a congressman, ambassador to the United Nations and mayor of

Atlanta, explained, "We wanted to do it illegally. . . . We want to be put in jail for furnishing heat and health requirements to people with children in the winter."[6]

From the start the seizure of the building was ill-thought-out or unthought-out. Editorial opinion was critical, which can sometimes be helpful but not when United States District Court judge James B. Parsons, an African American, called the taking of the building "theft." Nobody had done their homework. Andy Young did not get locked up "for furnishing heat and health requirements to people with children in the winter." Instead Mayor Daley sent out squads of building, health and fire inspectors in a show of cooperation with the slum-eradication campaign announced by the visiting ministers from the Southland. Municipal rat killers stalked the alleys of Lawndale hunting vermin. It was all very Kabuki and ineffectual.

As the organizational effort fizzled, King fell back on the tactic which had done so well in the South. He marched. He marched into several southwest side white communities and it was awful. It looked like the entire population, man, woman and child, was out on the lawns of their precisely cared-for Chicago vernacular bungalows, a stone in each hand and a curse in each mouth. Even the cops were getting hit, as was Dr. King himself. I had seen him stoned a few days before in front of the courthouse in Philadelphia, Mississippi, and, bad as that was, the howling and screeched obscenities in Chicago were worse. In the end the march accomplished nothing except to reinforce the perception among both blacks and whites that he was an outsider, heroic for some and hateful for others but an outsider.

SIX

ROCHESTER, NEW YORK, AND FIGHT; THE FAMOUS FART-IN;
RUMPELSTILTSKIN POLITICS; THE IMPORTANCE OF SAVING
THE OTHER GUY'S FACE; NOTHING'S NONNEGOTIABLE;
PROXIES FOR PEOPLE; JIMMY HOFFA

B y contrast, when four or five years before 1961 an Alinsky organization in the Woodlawn section of the city's black south
side had pulled a rent strike against a landlord, they knew who the
landlord was and they had a plan to circumnavigate the illegality
of what they were doing by putting rents in an escrow account
pending the settlement of the dispute.

Prior to the strike the Alinsky organization had demonstrated
its strength by registering voters and carrying out other activities
which had shown local politicians that it had the kind of power
which can be troublesome on election day. Thus, the politicians
were happy to do the organization a favor.

When the landlords went to court, though the law was on
their side, they faced a hostile, politically controlled judge who
had been instructed to grant the striking tenants postponements

from now to the end of time. It was a case of justice delayed, justice done. Realizing they would grow old and gray before their
case was heard, the landlords sat down to negotiate.

King's weakness in making a threat he was unable to carry out
illustrated another of Saul's beliefs: the best threats are made by
anonymously inserting them into the other side's imagination.

Which is what Alinsky did when in 1965 the IAF went into
Rochester, New York, then a thriving high-wage, high-tech city,
home base to both Kodak and Xerox. The city had been ripped
apart by race rioting and Alinsky had been approached by a
group of ministers, who had previously tried to interest Dr. King
in coming to their city; when that didn't work out the Southern
Christian Leadership Conference suggested Alinsky, who told
the ministers that he would require a biracial invitation. In addition, the Rochesterians would have to raise the money needed
to do the organizing.[1]

In the attempt to make these arrangements, Rochester was
torn in two, arguing over whether Alinsky should be invited at
all. If the argument had been settled by both sides coming together to issue a joint invitation, I doubt that Saul would have
accepted. He would have refused to come, not because he was
wedded to divisiveness, as he is often accused of, but because
when you have unanimity before the fact, before people are organized and have their own power lever, before they have
framed their agenda, there could be no change, no reform, no
progress. Unanimity is for after the struggle has been waged, the
negotiations concluded, the disagreements resolved, for the
handshaking, the ribbon cutting and the group pictures.

Alinsky could be a combative man. He never backed away from a fight he thought he could win if fighting was necessary, but he warned against making implacable enemies. He taught that you should conduct yourself even in the worst of brawls so that the other side could save face. Do not trap people, he would say. They have to have a back door to ease out of because all tussles must come to an end, most often around a negotiating table.

Along the same lines Saul warned about trapping yourself. You may need a back door as much as the other side. Hence, bellicose announcements of "nonnegotiable demands" and "deal breakers" were anathema to him. Unconditional surrender made sense to Saul when it was Franklin Roosevelt backed up by thirteen million men in arms in World War II; otherwise, he considered demanding it lunacy.

Fight as though you are 100 percent right, knowing that half the time you're lucky if you are only 49 percent wrong. Stay cool, keep your ego out of it and remember there must be an end game. Saul was known to harp on the disastrous places leaders' egos can take an organization or an issue, as a decent compromise is turned down because they want to look like the big winner.

For Alinsky, the archetypal example of petulant ego decision making of the period was Bill Ayers in his salad days, decades before he met Barack Obama. Ayers, the son of a rich Chicago corporate executive, was part of the Weather Underground, a minuscule group of collegians whose opposition to the Vietnam War took them into a comic-book leftism whose principal feature was anger at a government which did not do as they bade it. Their foot-stamping anger and humiliation at their failures at organizing and influencing current events made them believe they were justified in taking up violence. It was a tantrum or Rumpelstiltskin politics which included bomb throwing without the Taliban's skill with explosives. Before their run was completed Ayers's girlfriend and several others with whom he worked blew themselves up assembling explosive devices in a Greenwich Village row house.

Alinsky's first Rochester move was to send in his top organizer, Edward Chambers, a white man, who proceeded quietly to meet with scores of leading African Americans. Before going ahead he needed to know what were the items on the black Rochesterian list of things to be changed. A working committee was formed and it elected its leader and spokesman, a fiery black minister, Franklin Florence, who was of two minds about white people, which was helpful because the last thing needed was a suspicion that the organization aborning was a hand-puppet deal. It helped that the new group named itself FIGHT for Freedom—Independence—God—Honor—Today.

When Alinsky himself, who was viewed on the local editorial pages as an advanced scout for the Paris Commune, went to Rochester, his arrival made a large splash in the local media but not so large as to obliterate FIGHT. From the start it was clear that the IAF and FIGHT were two separate organizations, albeit working closely together until FIGHT was able to drop its training wheels and go its own way.

At the start of the Rochester organization drive Alinsky was a controversial figure. He had too much of a wise-guy reputation and the adjectives applied to him—"tough," "shrewd," "arrogant," and "clever"—were ones which win more admiration than affection. He made only a single statement that probably caused more panic and confusion among Rochester's power elite than anything months of protesting, picketing and getting arrested might have gained. Saul's index finger had an unerring ability to find the weak spot. In this case it was the Rochester Philharmonic, the cultural institution around which the city's fanciest and richest rotated in their pride and pretensions.

He told the Rochester media who were already in shaky emotional shape that instead of picket lines and sit-ins FIGHT's members in their best bibs and tuckers would gather at a supper preparatory to an evening of musical appreciation. Baked beans and nothing but baked beans would be served. As the beans did what beans do FIGHT's increasingly gaseous music-loving members would hie themselves to the concert hall where they would sit expelling gastrointestinal vapors with such noisy velocity as to compete with the woodwinds.

Saul had a high old time with the fart-in, as much of Rochester and beyond laughed at the pompous, petrified upper crust which ran the city. The fart-in, of course, never took place, nor was there need for it to be carried out, but the story has so conspicuously adhered to his memory that some people have the impression that the job description of an organizer's work is that of a merry prankster or frat house social director. It isn't.

The "fart-in" or "flatulent blitzkrieg," Saul explained, was "completely outside the city fathers' experience." Civil disobedience or rioting they were braced for but not this. It was with jabs such as this that Saul was able to bait his far more powerful opponents into making an angry lunge, whereupon he could by use of "political jujitsu" turn the other side's strength against itself. It helps if one has Saul's off-kilter genius which enabled him to be funny with serious intent.

The reaction to the threat of the "flatulent blitzkrieg" was so successful and so delighted Saul he told me that he was going to try a "piss-in" at O'Hare Airport in Chicago, which was perhaps closest to Mayor Daley's heart and pride. I told him that I thought that was one bathroom joke too many. I added that nobody in their right mind could believe you could pull a stunt like that off but once you have a reputation like Saul's people think you can do anything.

Saul said he would arrange to bring a large number of black people to O'Hare International Airport where they would occupy the urinals and toilet cubicles for as long as it takes. The African Americans taking part in this would all be dressed to the nines, looking as respectable as you can look, but in that period the mere appearance of a person of color was enough to set off social panic among whites. In point of fact it would not have been easy to recruit people for such a stunt, but Saul understood it would not come to that.

The piss-in idea never made it into full public view. Saul simply let it be known via a couple of city hall flunkies that he was thinking about clogging up what was then the world's busiest airport. That, he said, was enough to bring the city to the bargaining table.

For every positive, as Saul would say, there is a negative. That was one of his favorite lines and with the beans episode the negative is that to this day many think that "Alinsky tactics" are fraternity house stunts or public relations arpeggios. Tactics which are not integrated with and thematically connected with a large effort soon roll off without enduring effect and may even backfire.

The oblique nonthreat threat was how Saul operated. Whenever the topic would come up he would repeat: never make a threat you are not able to carry out and even if you can carry it out, don't do it. His reasoning was that regardless of how much damage you might do to the other side by carrying out the threat, it would be less than the damage the opponents had imagined you could do.

Part of the Rochester campaign was a struggle with the Kodak corporation to get what was then a worldwide corporate giant to hire African Americans living in their home city. In the face of a deviously obdurate management that confused doing the right thing with black outsiders intruding on their business, Saul was driven to new tactical expedients. It was during this fight that "proxies for people," collecting proxies to use to vote against corporate officers, was first attempted. Had Saul lived longer, he would have done much to organize what had become the powerless middle class by forcing change through proxies and other tactics.

Even while the Rochester battle was going on he was talking about getting thousands of people to buy one share each of a corporation and bring those thousands of shares to the annual meeting. Visions of a Yankee Stadium full of corporate stakeholders had taken hold of his imagination. As nutty as these visions may sound there is historical precedent for Saul's imaginings. Around

1930 A. P. Gianini, founder and CEO of the Bank of America, did something similar to that which Saul had in mind. Several hundred thousand ordinary people to whom he had sold stock in the bank rallied to his side in a war against the Wall Street interests who were trying to crush the San Francisco banker.

Saul's constant search for new ways to find and apply power brought him to at least one meeting with Jimmy Hoffa, the Teamsters Union president. If Hoffa is remembered at all today it is as the archetypal crooked labor leader whom Bobby Kennedy, when he was attorney general in his brother's administration, brought to justice. It did not help Hoffa's posthumous reputation that he was kidnaped and believed to have been murdered by one or another branch of organized crime.

The real Hoffa story is more complicated. The man, whatever his gangster connections, was a militant trade unionist, a talented organizer and a labor leader who brought significant wage increases and other benefits to his rank-and-file membership. He also, like Saul, was interested in organizing the new white-collar masses. From what I remember Saul telling me about their conversation, some kind of collaboration would have been possible.

Saul gave the Hoffa idea a lot of thought. After signing an agreement to train and hire some hundreds of FIGHT members, virtually all-white Kodak had an internal battle over integration and the all-whites inside the corporation won. In the battle against the company a Teamsters Union refusal to cross a civil rights picket line might have finally forced the corporate behemoth to embrace the equal opportunity employment policy it was not going to institute of its own volition. There was a real possibility of shutting Kodak down, but it would have involved a highly publicized partnership with what a lot of people would have considered organized crime. Saul more than anybody understood the near impossibility of winning a strike or a fight such as this one if public sympathy and support turned against you. In the end he decided that the heat a working alliance with Hoffa would have brought down on the IAF and its projects was too high a price to pay.

SEVEN

LEWIS TEACHES ALINSKY HUMOR AS A TACTIC; SAUL AND
JOHN L. PIG OUT AT CAFÉ CHAMBORD; THE PLUSES AND MI-
NUSES OF PUTTING COMMIES ON THE PAYROLL; BORROW-
ING VAN BITTNER'S GOON SQUAD; HANK JOHNSON
MURDERED OUT OF GRATITUDE; THE HOT DOG–FILET
MIGNON CONTINUUM; IF YOU START AN ORGANIZATION,
DON'T JOIN IT

I t was around 1939 while he was organizing the Back of the Yards
that Saul began his long association with John L. Lewis (1880–
1969). Lewis was the president of the United Mine Workers, a
union of perhaps a half-million members with a long and violent
history in an industry as famous for its bloody strikes as for its terrible accidents. Although today few people have heard of him, in
the 1930s Lewis was a huge figure on the American scene, as well
known in that decade as Martin Luther King was in the 1960s.
Those living in a service/consumption society must stretch their
imaginations to picture the dirty, bloody, laborious, dangerous coal
mining life which Lewis grew up in. There is nothing like it in the
United States today.

Thundering his battle cry, "Organize the unorganized!" Lewis had provided the direction and the impetus for the Congress of Industrial Organizations, the feared CIO. Using the Mine Workers' treasury, Lewis hired organizers to start unions in the rubber, automobile, steel, meatpacking and electrical industries. By the time he was done he had played a leading part in enrolling several million industrial workers. In four or five years he had laid the foundation for the transformation of the economic and social landscape of the country. The middle-class life, the loss of which the nation was to suffer with the crash of 2007, came about in no small measure thanks to the organizational drives started by Lewis. In his time millions of industrial workers looked to him as their leader.

Although his work with gangsters had enabled Saul to study power politics at a municipal level—as it was played with shootings, jailings and corrupt goings-on—Lewis was working on a much larger stage where baseball bats, the simple passing of money and the Thompson submachine gun (known colloquially as "the Chicago piano") did not suffice.

Alinsky's association with Lewis taught him the tactics of humor, surprise and theatrics on a national stage. He doted on narrating stories of how Lewis brought the largest corporations in the world and the most powerful politicians to their knees.

One of Saul's favorite yarns concerned Lewis's meeting with the General Motors negotiating team. This was when GM was the world's largest and most successful industrial corporation. The negotiation came only after months of paralyzing sit-down strikes, mass picketing, intervention by the National Guard, sporadic violence, injunctions, police billy clubs and what had become a national crisis.

The meeting took place in a grand room furnished with a long table. GM's chief negotiator sat in the middle, flanked on either side by twenty-five or so lawyers, accountants and lesser executives. Lewis was about to enter the room with his group of five or six men when he saw GM seated in all its serried importance. Lewis turned quickly to his small group and told them to wait outside. Then Lewis with his gigantic jowled face and cantilevered eyebrows walked alone and without briefcase to the long table, took his seat opposite the General Motors bosses and said in his basso voice, "Let us begin."

Studying the tactics Lewis used during conflicts between the unarmed strikers and their families and the National Guard, the courts, the newspapers, the bankers and the police gave Saul the rudiments of some of the ideas that later he perfected, polished and published in *Rules for Radicals*.

Once in a while Saul would fall into a Lewis reminiscence mood. He would tell how, when the union boss was in New York, he ate at Café Chambord on Third Avenue, said to be the most expensive restaurant in the city and a proper setting for someone of Lewis's imperial stature. As I heard Saul tell the story, he and Lewis were there when an army private and his girlfriend came in, looked at the menu and were shocked by the prices. The couple shared a cheese sandwich and left. In their wake, the two men wondered whether given such prices it would be possible to spend as much as one hundred dollars on a dinner (the equivalent of perhaps two thousand dollars in today's money). Neither of them were able to reach the goal.

It was out of character for Saul to spend that much money on a meal, but he was with a man whom he was close to idolizing.

He also had more than a passing interest in how those with limitless bank accounts (in Lewis's case the union treasury) spent money. He told me that Lewis got his clothes at A. Sulka, a men's haberdashery that was where toffs such as the Duke of Windsor were supposed to have bought their togs. In those days Sulka's Chicago store was next to the IAF office at 8 South Michigan and Saul and I would window-shop the ties. But I was the one who bought something there—the bright red vest with gold buttons which I later wore when I was organizing on Chicago's southwest side. It was on sale at a deep discount, perhaps because anyone staring at it for more than a few seconds was forced to look away and blink.

Saul wrote a biography of Lewis which was close to being a love letter, albeit one with much information about the union leader's life not available elsewhere (*John L. Lewis: An Unauthorized Biography*). The book contained passages that tiptoed up to various incidents only to swerve away from the whole truth. In describing Lewis's relationship with Samuel Gompers, the founder of the American Federation of Labor, who with Lewis and Walter Reuther was one of the three most important figures in the history of American unionism, Saul wrote, "They became intimate friends. Gompers trusted Lewis implicitly, and it is reliably reported that whenever Gompers would go on a carouse he would trust Lewis to stand guard against any unfavorable repercussions."[1] In Lewis-reminiscence mood, Saul said that actually Gompers would post the large and very tough Lewis in front of Gompers' hotel room door so the older man could safely while away the night making merry with a string of hookers.

Lewis told Saul that Gompers would have three women a night. Whether or not that impressed John L., it impressed Saul who was not given to the aimless vulgarities of locker room talk.

The real reason the labor leader was standing guard outside of Gompers' hotel room was not the only thing which did not make it into the Lewis biography. Lewis and President Franklin Roosevelt had worked together throughout the decade of the 1930s, despite their not being able to stand each other. But by 1940 Lewis was moving toward breaking with Roosevelt who was trying to galvanize the country to join the fight against Hitler. Many Americans had little interest in being galvanized into signing up for a foreign war. They had fought one fewer than twenty-five years before and believed that it was politicians' lies that had tricked them into going "over there" in 1917.

Lewis was one such. He was not only an isolationist but fearful that Roosevelt would use his wartime powers to smash the labor movement, as he thought Woodrow Wilson had done in World War I. Even without a war, he feared that organized labor was in danger of being converted into an appendage of the Democratic Party to the detriment of labor's independence. Saul argued with Lewis, saying that if the labor leader opposed Roosevelt's run for a third term, he would be left politically weightless with no candidate and in the company of the Communist Party with its pro-Hitler-Stalin, anti-Roosevelt position.

Saul himself was strongly against the fascists and in the Roosevelt war camp. Though he sympathized with Lewis's antipathy to the expanding power of the central government, he was a Roosevelt supporter through and through. He looked on a split between the two men as a calamity. To prevent it Saul arranged two meetings for the chieftains to compose their differences. During the second, in Roosevelt's White House bedroom, Lewis accused the president of having ordered the FBI to tap his phone. The president denied it, which so infuriated Lewis that he slammed out of the executive mansion to tell a waiting Alinsky, "No man can call John L. Lewis a liar, and least of all, FDR!"

Some people have doubted the story but Saul was a teller of yarns, not a spinner of them. Not only did he write that story, but I heard him tell it more than once. The details never varied and the most fantastic things which Saul said would turn out to be true.

Alinsky eventually came to believe that Lewis "lived 20 years too long," but he described the union leader in his prime in the 1930s as "the old Napoleonic master of power and strategy: cold, ruthless, ingenious."[2] Saul became a confidant of Lewis's and an adviser or as much of one as the man's dictatorial personality would tolerate. Although the labor leader was almost thirty years older than his young apprentice in the study of power, they grew to be good-enough friends that Lewis, Saul said, wanted him to marry his daughter, Kathryn, a rotund woman with her father's smarts and, unluckily, his looks. Saul's admiration for Lewis, however, did not extend so far although Kathryn did become a member of the Industrial Areas Foundation board.

Some historians have questioned the closeness of the Lewis-Alinsky relationship in the course of doubting some of the statements in Alinsky's biography. But whenever Saul was in Washington he would see Lewis. And I remember "Mr. Lewis" calling Saul every once in a while and the two of them chatting about politics. Saul was deferential but not in the way he reserved for potential sources of money. This was the deference reserved for those you are close to and respect.

Despite the many Lewis stories which Saul told with such dramatic vividness and detail that you could see yourself in yesteryear's tumultuous battles for decent pay and dignity, there was one he neither wrote about nor told. He asked me not to repeat it, though he couldn't resist passing it on. Now, so many years later and with those concerned long since dead, I doubt he'd mind my telling what I still remember.

It took place around the time Lewis had decided he was done with Roosevelt but was worried that the rupture might make it look as if he were following the Communist line. When he had fired up the juggernaut which unionized America's basic industries, there hadn't been enough talent among his United Mine Workers to organize drives on such a scale. Once he had assigned his best people, the only pool of intelligent, fired-up, energetic organizers to be found were among the Communists. For Lewis it was Communist organizers or no organizers. The trick was to take the *Daily Worker* (the Communist newspaper) out of their coat pockets so people did not know who they were. It was a balancing act: when their goals were the same as yours, there were none better and when their goals were different, there were none more disloyal.

Saul may have explained to me why Lewis decided certain men were so dangerous something had to be done about them but if so I cannot remember it. Suffice it to say, according to

Alinsky, Lewis did decide that they had to be removed from their union positions at once. Trying to extract them by voting them out at the local union level or at annual conventions would have been the political equivalent of working a barbed spear from your flesh.

Saul related that Lewis wanted him to supervise the job. He would be given temporary direction of Van Bittner's goon squad. Bittner, whom *Time* once called Lewis's "no. 1 soapbox fireball," was, when off the podium, soft-spoken but more dangerous. Goon squads do not leave a paper trail but here and there you can get a whiff. A Communist Party document talking about the Little Steel Strike of 1937 contains en passant this paragraph: "Aaron Cohen had been a coal miner in southern Illinois and a leader in the reform movement of the United Mine Workers of America. As such, he earned the wrath of one Van A. Bittner, UMWA district director, whose goons once beat Aaron within an inch of his life."[3]

Thus equipped Saul visited five or six midwestern cities where the men on Lewis's list were given the choice of leaving town or finding themselves in an "ash can." I remember Saul's use of the term "ash can" even when other details of the story have been forgotten.

Resort to political violence here in America seems inexcusable in the first decades of the twenty-first century, but in 1940 it was all too possible that Hitler might extinguish democracy in much of the world. If Communists in key union positions in strategic industries were thinking of helping the fascist cause, Alinsky would do whatever he could to thwart them. Saul's unforgiving antifascism explains why he undertook the job.

For Alinsky the Communists were a thorny problem. Many of them, but not all, were the servants of an antidemocratic foreign power and an outsider could not tell who were the loyal Americans and who were not. Both the loyal and disloyal were often intelligent, resourceful and very useful, so though Saul had no relationship with the party itself he did associate with individual party members. It was a tangle of inconsistencies necessary because of the times and circumstances, but Saul was never phased by inconsistencies. When asked why he had never joined the Communist Party, he would say, "I didn't join because I had a sense of humor."

Hank Johnson was one party member with whom Saul was very close. Johnson was an African American whom Alinsky ranked as one of the very best organizers. Johnson worked for the Packinghouse Workers Organizing Committee and was with Alinsky when he was putting the Back of the Yards Neighborhood Council together. Aside from being one of those rare persons who could talk with and get along with anybody, Johnson was an outstanding orator. Johnson told Saul he wanted to get out of the party, but that, while easier to do than withdrawing from the Mafia, could be difficult. Nevertheless, Saul helped Johnson extricate himself by arranging with Lewis to put him on the Mine Workers' payroll.

Johnson had a sidekick, Arthur Shelton, a perpetual foul-up who was always getting into trouble and whom Johnson always rescued. As Alinsky told the story, Shelton owed Johnson for so many rescues and favors that his gratitude turned into resentment and then hatred. Hank either didn't notice or chose to ignore his friend's growing bitterness. He stepped in once more to save Shelton when he botched up negotiations with an Indiana utility company. Claiming that Johnson had set up the rescue operation to humiliate him, Shelton filed a formal complaint with their mutual boss, the United Mine Workers Union. A hearing on the matter was convened. Shelton testified and when the hearing officer asked if he had anything else to offer, Shelton replied, "I just want to make one more point," reached into his briefcase, pulled out a gun and murdered his friend.[4]

Johnson's death hit Alinsky hard. Twenty years later he was still bringing up his friend's name and remarking what a loss and what a waste it was. More than that, it gave Saul the text to talk on a theme he would often come back to—the humiliation recipients feel toward those who help them. For Saul the story was not just about the loss of his friend. It was proof of the trouble which comes of giving people what they ought to have a chance to earn for themselves.

For Alinsky it was another contradiction. He was devoting a lifetime to trying to give others a chance to stand alone and decide things for themselves. The gift lays people under a heavy obligation to the giver and reveals the conundrum of the relationship between the leader and the led.

The led are seldom satisfied. Saul used to say that as soon as the fight for hot dogs is won, the led want hamburger and after they get hamburger, they want steak. There comes a point when even the most successful leaders are unable to deliver more. As that point nears, the followers begin preparations for putting the leader in a pot as a tasty substitute for the filet mignon the leader can't deliver. Either that or the leader tries to turn the followers into obedient political robots.

The hot dog–filet mignon continuum describes the relationship only at a material level. It does not deal with the psychic at-your-throat-or-at-your-knees connection between the leader and led. That concerns gratitude and resentment, hero worship and hero disillusionment, ego and who gets the recognition, the perks and the power. Such tensions and rivalries are supposed to be relieved and adjusted by the democratic succession of leaders, but Saul would point out that most organizations quickly develop an old guard with calcified vested interests.

Saul saw in Lewis's career and that of others the arching pathway up from dynamic beginnings to the apogee of accomplishment to sclerotic organizational dementia. We used to talk about what might be done to postpone or mitigate it. Saul's half-facetious idea was to build a time bomb into a new organization set to go off in five years. Needless to say, we were unable to invent such a device, but playing with the thought indicates how much the master organizer distrusted organizations, but then Saul, à la Groucho Marx, used to say that he never started an organization he cared to join.

EIGHT

ALINSKY AND THE MARTIN LUTHER (NOT KING) MOVIE;
SAUL AND THE ROMAN CATHOLIC CHURCH; BISHOP
BERNARD SHEIL; ROTTEN-EGG SYNDROME; SAUL CAN'T
FIND THE RACETRACK; ALINSKY PLAYS DUENNA; BISHOP
SHEIL ACCUSES ALINSKY OF SELLING OUT TO THE CATHOLIC
CHURCH

When Saul began organizing, luck favored him in one respect. George Mundelein, the cardinal archbishop of
Chicago, was, unlike many of his fellow bishops, a New Deal supporter and an antifascist sympathetic to Franklin Roosevelt's foreign policy. The American Catholic Church then and now are
unrecognizably different. Then priests and laymen alike, when en-
tering the presence of the cardinal archbishop, would genuflect and
kiss his jeweled episcopal ring. Inside the mansion on North State
Parkway where the cardinal lived, there was a throne room. If cardinals were the princes of the church, none were more so than His
Eminence, George Cardinal Mundelein, who, when visiting parish
churches, prefaced his entrance with a trumpeted fanfare. He was

a tall man, well over six feet, who appointed equally tall men to the most important administrative posts in the archdiocese. His retinue of giants enhanced the powerful shadow his image cast. During his reign it seemed as though Chicago lived under the divided rule of Al Capone and George Mundelein, whose limousine with its Illinois 1 license plates moved through the city streets with a police motorcycle escort.

Among the Protestant and Jewish minority, Mundelein's displays of medieval pageantry reinforced their centuries-old opinions about papist antidemocratic ambitions, but the Catholic Church of the first three-quarters of the twentieth century was obliviously involved with itself. In 1926 Mundelein arranged for his fellow American cardinals in the Atlantic seaboard and another six or seven from Rome to come to Chicago in a special train painted red and gold, there to sit on their thrones while mass was said for an estimated one million attendees.

In the years when Alinsky was most active in Chicago the thought of getting on the wrong side of the Catholic Church was terrifying for a politician or interest group. The church could boycott you, order their members to vote against you or pull their money from your institution. It seldom if ever did any of those things openly. Instead it operated through the archdiocese's lawyers, Kirkland, Fleming, Green, Martin & Ellis, which also represented the *Chicago Tribune* in the era of its glory. Whenever the Chancery Office (the executive offices of the diocese) wanted something done or not done the request came not from the Catholic Church but from Kirkland, Fleming, the powerhouse Protestant law firm.

Thus power was wielded but nobody could prove it was the Catholic Church behind what had been done. There was no paper trail, nothing except that not-to-be-mentioned whispered call from Kirkland, Fleming. On one occasion the call was made to the area's movie theater owners. A movie about the life of Martin Luther (not King) had come out but it did not sit well with the archdiocese that a film glorifying the grand heretic would show in the Greater Chicago area. The Kirkland, Fleming phone call was made and no movie house within maybe a hundred miles of the city had room on its schedule for Martin Luther.

Liberals and Protestant churchmen were furious. In those circles Alinsky was considered the cat's paw of the papacy. We were accused of trying to maintain the black ghetto to protect the church's real estate interests, which were immense. There were dozens of parishes, parochial schools, hospitals and so forth that would be surrounded by a black population if the people hemmed in behind the ghetto's walls were allowed to buy homes in nearby white communities. There was no truth in it but it was hard to get cooperation from those who believed we were the tools of this conspiracy.

Such suspicions might have been allayed but for many non-Catholics of the period, Protestant, Jewish or agnostic, talking to a priest or—ye gods!—a nun was a rare, somewhat embarrassing encounter. For them Catholic America was an ill-lit land and the church a quasi-military, quasi-royal organization whose members, when issued an order, genuflected and obeyed.

They refused to believe the Catholic Church was a complicated institution riven with factions, warring opinions, conflicting interest groups and feuding nationalities whose antagonisms toward each other could be more intense than any felt toward non-Catholics.

When word got out that Martin Luther would not appear on area screens, I started getting my ribs kicked in. The work was tough enough without getting stung every day by angry WASPs and civil libertarians. The civil libertarian part of Saul agreed with the attackers but he was a believer in keeping things simple and, beyond all else, keeping attention on what you were trying to do. As far as he was concerned there were plenty of people to protest and carry on about a movie and it was a diversion from what we were supposed to be doing.

I kept whining and nagging to no avail until Alinsky indicated he might—no promises, but he might—bring it up with Ed Burke, the chancellor. We were scheduled to have dinner with several of the heavyweight monsignors, including Burke and Vincent Cook, the head of Catholic Charities and the man who, when the cardinal said so, wrote the checks which paid for much of what Alinsky was doing.

We met at Barney's Market Club, a steak house patronized by Chicago's more important politicians, grafters, paving contractors and political priests. The restaurant where Barney greeted every customer with a booming, "Yes, sir, senators!" was thick with cigar smoke in that long-ago time before lung cancer or cholesterol had been invented. That evening at the table with the two powerful monsignors, nobody paid. Barney, as always, picked up the tab. After the thick slabs of roast beef and sour cream–topped baked potatoes had made their way down our respective gullets, Saul turned to Burke to say, "Ed, this Luther movie—"

"Saul, it's done. He was an apostate."

"Well, it's causing a lot of trouble, and I have a solution."

"You do?"

"Yeah, let them show the movie."

"No!"

"Ed, hear me out. Let them play the movie but with one stipulation. They have to show it backwards. That way Martin Luther ends up a Catholic!"

Burke let out a guffaw before he said, "Saul, you're a son of a bitch." And with that another call was made to Kirkland, Fleming, and as mysteriously as the movie was banned, it was unbanned.

Saul was relaxed and at home with Catholics right up the hierarchical scale to cardinal. He had known Catholics from the time he was little, living behind the family tailor shop in the Maxwell Street ghetto. The Roman Catholic Shabbat goy who lit the Sabbath lights in the Orthodox homes of Saul's childhood turned up years later as the rector of Chicago's Holy Name Cathedral.

The gangs and gangsters he came to know as a criminologist were of Catholic origins and, of course, the Back of the Yards was one of those classic Chicago Catholic neighborhoods. Closed worlds of their own, parochial, safe, protective and comforting and very, very Catholic were those communities. Time was when in a parish such as St. Sabina's on the southwest side people would drop to their knees on the sidewalk of Racine Avenue as an altar boy tinkling a small bell walked by. He would be followed by a priest in cassock and surplice on his way to a sick call holding a pyx containing the Eucharistic wafer.

Saul's long and complicated relationship with the Roman Catholic Church was indispensable to many of his achievements even as it was often a hindrance. Whether it helped or hurt it was an inexplicable contradiction for the many people who had both Saul and the Catholic Church typecast to the point they could not understand either.

I don't think that Saul ever met Cardinal Mundelein but as the Back of the Yards Council began to come into existence, he did meet Bernard Sheil, one of Mundelein's auxiliary bishops, a vocal, hair-up-the-ass liberal anomaly in the conservative American Catholic hierarchy of the 1930s, a man who became a national figure, presumably with the liberally inclined but less vocal Mundelein's concurrence.

In 1939 Cardinal Mundelein died and Bishop Sheil mobilized his connections in both the under- and overworlds to help him move up from auxiliary bishop to archbishop. President Roosevelt did his best via back-burner diplomacy to push the cause of America's most politically liberal Catholic bishop.

Even though Sheil was not *the* bishop of Chicago, he was a man with a national name as well as being from the largest diocese in the United States. A Catholic bishop could be a luminary then in a way hard for us to imagine now. It was in the era when tens of millions were in the pews every Sunday and every holy day of obligation, when the seminaries were bursting with students, when thousands of women were nuns, when the laity listened to the Catholic clergy with reverence and obeyed.

Sheil's importance transcended that of his ecclesiastic office. His name became nationally known after he started the Catholic Youth Organization in 1930. With boxing tournaments and like activities the CYO, and by extension Sheil himself, was everywhere. The Catholic Church in America and the bishop both reached their zenith sometime in the middle years of the last century. But Sheil's zenith was not high enough to satisfy him. He was a textbook example of a type of political, celebrity, sports-world priest not seen anymore and he wanted to be an archbishop, although once he had been told by a banker that he had kicked away his chances.

Time magazine reported the incident:

> The banker was astonished at the bishop. It was 1939, the packinghouse workers were on the verge of striking for recognition of their C.I.O. union, and here was the Most Rev. Bernard James Sheil, senior auxiliary bishop of Chicago's Roman Catholic archdiocese, accepting "as a great privilege" the invitation of John L. Lewis to appear on a C.I.O. platform in the stockyard district. "I want you to remember, Your Excellency," said the banker, a Catholic layman, "that the minute you step on that platform, you lose your chance to become archbishop."
>
> For a moment, the stubby little prelate just looked at him. "You should know," he said after a while, "that I wasn't ordained a Catholic priest in order to become an archbishop."[1]

It fell to Saul to prove the banker wrong. I have no dates for this but it must have been around 1940 after Cardinal Mundelein died and the Chicago See fell vacant. A third party, possibly Mob connected or one of the businessmen backing Sheil, came to Saul to tell him Sheil had an errand for him. He

was to hie himself to Rome to put in the fix for Sheil's elevation
to the archbishopric of Chicago. In terms of ecclesiastic prefer-
ment, Chicago, home to more Catholics than any other place in
the United States, was the plum of plums.

To ensure Sheil's appointment, Saul was to deliver a packet
containing, if I recall correctly, fifty thousand dollars, a very
large sum in Depression-decade dollars.

It was a wild story, but though Saul was known to exaggerate
when his audience was looking especially bright eyed and bushy
tailed he did not invent tales from scratch. The money was to be
taken to a monastery concealed from the twentieth century
somewhere in the Apennines in Abruzzi. Whether Saul was to
place the money in a particular person's hands or leave it behind
three loose stones twenty paces from the north gate of the wall,
I cannot remember. Nor can I be sure that he made the trip. It
didn't matter, because as Saul said, he took the money and he
returned the money. The young organizer found neither person
nor place to deposit it. Loud-spoken Bernie Sheil, whose name
was so tarnished by controversy he never had a realistic shot at
the job, was passed over for a man whose political and social
views were not so different from Sheil's but who was circum-
spect about airing them in public.

Saul's conclusion was that when you want to fix a horse race
you drive out to the track and you bribe a jockey, but when you
try to bribe the Vatican, you can't even find the racetrack.

The Chicago job went to Samuel Cardinal Stritch, whom Sheil
seems to have hated from the moment the new man hit town.

In the early days Sheil was indispensable to Alinsky. He passed
the word in the Back of the Yards that this Jewish agnostic was

okay, which at least ensured that he would not be kicked out the door. Sheil did not have the power, the prestige or the respect in those foreign-language parishes to do more. Saul used to say that in such situations the approval of a bishop or a pastor got you nothing but a hunting license to try to organize the members of the parish.

Saul's relationship with the bishop was political and organizational. They believed in unions, they believed in organizing people so that they could better themselves and their communities and they were both committed antifascists in a period when fascism of either the Italian or the German stripe had an appeal which twenty-first-century Americans would find incomprehensible. If it hadn't been for Sheil Saul might have remained a unique talent without the means of fulfilling its potential. Sheil it was who introduced Alinsky to Marshall Field III, whose fortune was counted in the hundreds of millions in those days and who provided the young propounder of fresh ideas and a propensity for kicking up controversy with the money to sustain himself and start on his unique career.

Saul had his uses for Sheil, helping to keep him in the limelight that his all-about-me personality needed. Speaking out on subjects Catholic bishops did not discuss brought Sheil some of the notoriety necessary for him, but being connected to Saul's attention-getting activities earned him attention also. Saul was grateful to the bishop and, though they were not close, he was loyal to him.

Bernie Sheil was one of several Dorian Gray personalities who trooped through Alinsky's life. The liberal crusader for the working man lived the way anti-Catholics have always said the clergy lives out of the laity's sight. He carried on as his friend Marshall Field III did, though without Field's money. Sheil's grand standard of living came from the collection box and grew more conspicuous until his embezzlements reached such a scale Cardinal Stritch retired him from the directorships of the charitable organizations from which this advocate for the underdog scooped such a rich existence. The career arcs of leaders gone sour were a frequent subject of meditation for Saul, one complicated by his loyalty for comrades long past their zenith, showing the first symptoms of rotten-egg syndrome.

There were tales which Saul, who loved a good story, didn't tell. He did not talk about his having to act as a duenna to protect Bishop Sheil and another board member, Agnes Meyer (1887–1970), both of whom had been indispensable supporters of the work in the early days when Saul was feeling his way.

Meyer, the wife of the owner of the *Washington Post* and the mother of Katharine Graham, was a powerful prop, both in money raising and in publicity, and a pluperfect example of why Saul hated the kind of high-level begging he was forced to do to keep the operation alive.

If daughter Katharine was gifted, mother Agnes was brilliant. Born into a wiggy Lutheran family in which the children had to take daily ice baths to strengthen their morals, Agnes worked her way through Columbia University's Barnard College to become the first woman reporter on the *New York Sun* in 1907. After that she could be found studying at the Sorbonne and spending her idle hours with such as Constantin Brancusi, Darius Milhaud and Auguste Rodin. Her marriage did not slow her down, as she continued to write and study Chinese civilization at Columbia, producing her first book, *Chinese Painting as Reflected in the Thought and Art of Li Lung Mien*. She would later translate one of Thomas Mann's books from the German even as she wrote a broadly republished series in the *Washington Post* about the Back of the Yards Neighborhood Council. She was also a drunk and a wild woman.

The Meyers had an estate of baronial proportion at Mount Kisco, New York, where Agnes and the bishop wanted to while away the hours together in grove and garden. The seemliness of the two being alone would have caused talk, so Saul was pressed into service. While walking the grounds, he saw the two lovers strolling nearby. They were hand in hand, Sheil in his bishop's cassock, Agnes in the matching cassock she had had made for herself.

As an agnostic with a heavy smear of cynicism, Alinsky was resigned to Sheil's being one of those public moralists whose private lives are out of sync with their public ones. The contradiction did not hinder their working together. You could say that both had cut their teeth in the juvenile delinquency–youth work field. Both had come quickly to understand that baseball fields and basketball courts would not prevent one carjacking or gang shoot-out. Both came to believe that juvenile delinquency would diminish only when young people lived in a society which offered them the chance of a real job and a real life.

In the wild and chaotic days of the 1930s labor battles, Sheil was the only Catholic bishop in the United States to stand on a platform with John L. Lewis and back the CIO, the organizational vehicle which was bringing unions to America's heavy industries. It was during those times Sheil and Alinsky came

together and they stayed together through the formation of the
Back of the Yards Neighborhood Council. They were together
when Sheil took on Father Charles Coughlin, the radio priest
with millions of listeners, who as the 1930s rolled on changed
from a nativistic protofascist into an outright anti-Semite. They
were still together when Sheil was the only prominent Catholic
cleric to go on a public attack against McCarthyism and Senator
Joseph McCarthy himself.

In April 1954 the bishop appeared before more than two thousand members of the United Automobile Workers in Chicago's
Civic Opera House to denounce the "phony anti-Communism"
practiced by "the junior senator from Wisconsin." I am almost
sure Saul arranged Sheil's appearance. I know that he arranged
for massive media coverage. The speech was one of the first of
the avalanche of large boulders which did in "Tail Gunner Joe,"
as he was known to his admirers.[2]

The bishop courted publicity, though the story of his farm in
one of Chicago's tonier exurbs where he stabled his string of
polo ponies was kept out of the papers. Despite his years working with Saul, his hatred of Cardinal Stritch was such that when
Saul informed his board that the cardinal had made a major
grant to the IAF, Sheil and Agnes Meyer immediately resigned.

The bishop sent Saul a telegram in which he said, "YOU HAVE
SOLD OUT TO THE CATHOLIC CHURCH." This is not one of those stories. Saul showed me the telegram. He was not laughing at such
an accusation coming from a member of the Catholic hierarchy.
Sheil and Saul had been through much together from early organizing days through the worst of the McCarthy blizzard. Sheil

was a friend and, though Alinsky said nothing, the parting, I do believe, hurt him.

It came when Sheil was on the decline. His defalcations and baronial living off of church money had forced the archdiocese to move in on him, although the bishop did his best to make his eclipse look like the penalty he was paying for his opposition to Joe McCarthy. Soon Sheil, who was finally made an archbishop but with no diocese to go with it, slunk into the north side of Chicago, where he was the pastor and, as far as the great world was concerned, was not seen or heard from again. None of this would have mattered to Saul who did not abandon friends. Sheil was not the only person in Saul's life who had dipped into the honey pot without its affecting his friendship, but Sheil cut off all contact. As far as I know the two never spoke again.

NINE

ALINSKY'S ADVANCE MAN, MSGR. JOHN O'GRADY; IN-
TERETHNIC BATTLES; AH, THOSE FETISH PRIESTS; NOT SO-
CIAL WORK BUT SOCIAL CONTROL; WHITE-COLLAR
PINKERTONS; TORTURING THE PRISSY-PANTS PEOPLE

A lthough I suspect there was no love in the relationship between Sheil and Alinsky, he had a deep affection for Father
John O'Grady, whom he had met in the early 1940s, possibly introduced by Sheil. While Sheil was doing his best to get into the history books, O'Grady was making sure he stayed out of them. The
monsignor was content with his briefcase, his unflagging enthusiasm and his belief in finer tomorrows.

Although some liberals and some Protestants believed that
Saul had made a devil's compact with Rome, in actuality he
never had *the* Roman Catholic Church backing him, but only
some parts of it and Saul did not start out courting it. Until he
began organizing he had had no contact with Catholics to speak
of. The Jewish world and the Catholic world of Saul's boyhood
may have brushed shoulders, but they existed in different social

galaxies. The Irish-controlled Chicago Democratic Party was not welcoming to Jews until Saul was a college student in the late 1920s. He said that he remembered that as a small kid he heard the cries of the Polish Catholic girls being raped in Douglas Park by the Jewish boys. It sounds awful and because it was awful I have a clear memory of his telling me about it.

The viciousness and absoluteness of racial, religious and ethnic separation in the big cities of the first half of the twentieth century are unimaginable to some twenty-first-century Americans brought up on the ideals of diversity and sensitivity to others. Acts of such vicious wantonness practiced by members of one group on another have pretty much gone underground but like pollution from old factories every so often crimes of this kind bubble up into the open to stain the landscape even now.

To appreciate who Alinsky was and what he accomplished one must know how violent and unforgiving were the divisions between groups and subgroups. Americans are brought up to think in terms of powerful majority groups quashing minorities, as in whites exploiting blacks or straights hounding gays, but the actual history of intergroup relations is darker and more tangled. Arriving on Ellis Island with immigrants were all the Old World's religious, national and ethnic animosities and hatreds.

In the years leading up to World War II you might have heard a Jew of Eastern European origins tell a German Jew that Hitler served him right. Among Catholics, Old World nationality trumped Holy Mother Church in the archdiocese's struggle to impose English and unity on foreign-language parishes. At one point in the 1920s the cardinal had bulls of excommunication tacked up on the church doors of a number of insubordinate Polish pastors.

As late as the 1950s Msgr. Steve McMahon, the pastor of a Roman Catholic parish on the far southwest side of Chicago which was said to contain the homes of 90 percent of the city's police captains, explained that he could not countenance the possibility of a black family moving into the neighborhood because "it was only two years ago that we let the Dagos in." The idea of the monolithic Roman Catholic Church existed mostly in the imaginations of Catholic-fearing Protestants and agnostic liberals. In the nation Saul grew up in Methodist parents disowned their daughters if they married Baptist boys. Nor did Lithuanian boys marry Slovenian girls.

I remember being at a meeting with Bishop Burke of Buffalo and three powerful Polish pastors. The Poles were arguing with the bishop over who would control certain moneys. Finally one of the Polish monsignors got up, looked the bishop straight in the face and informed him, "No goddamn Irishman is going to tell me what to do!" With that the man slammed out of the room and the meeting was over.

In the early days when Saul was not only doing his first organizing but also thinking through its rationale, Bishop Sheil's help had been indispensable in putting together the Industrial Areas Foundation, which provided Saul with a living after he left his day job in the juvenile delinquency field. But it was his relationship with Father John O'Grady which became a close and rollicking friendship. As a major lobbyist for the Catholic Church from the Harding-Coolidge era through the New Deal period

into the Eisenhower administration and as the director of the
National Conference of Catholic Charities in Washington, D.C.,
the older man had contacts everywhere. He must have known
almost every bishop in America and every useful politician in
Washington.

In his prime there was scarcely anyone of use whom O'Grady
didn't have a book on. Acting as a sort of scout, he warned Saul
off the bad ones and paved the way where things looked promising. He worked on scaring up possible donors, booked Saul as
a speaker to influential groups, arranged meetings with useful
people and put in the fix where he could.

O'Grady had spent half a lifetime propagating a professional
approach to Roman Catholic social work. After watching Saul
Alinsky do his best to kick it to pieces, O'Grady reversed his position, wanting instead to deprofessionalize it and turn it back to
local control by the people in the pews. This change in O'Grady's
long-held beliefs seems to have been connected to a democratic
epiphany when he visited the Back of the Yards Council and saw
what can happen when people organize to gain power for themselves. Since, after the government, Catholic Charities was the
largest social service network in the country, this shift in view-
point by a man of O'Grady's position and prestige may have
played a part in the changes which began reshaping the profession in the 1970s.

O'Grady hated being a priest. He said his mother forced him
into the seminary. The Ireland he was born into was a poverty-
stricken nation in which becoming a priest was one of the few
paths for advancement. But there were too many priests, just as

there were too many of everybody else, so they were exported to be missionaries across the globe. The FBIs, or foreign-born Irish, were not always welcomed by the American-born clergy, but that division was but one more cleft, and a relatively minor one, in an American Roman Catholic Church riven by national and social fissures.

This young immigrant priest did not want to be stuck in a parish in a backwater town. I do not know how it came about, whether there was a shortage of priests there or it was an assignment O'Grady wangled himself so that he had ecclesiastic permission to stay in America, but he ended up in the diocese of Omaha, Nebraska, where he may have talked the bishop into letting him go off to study or the bishop may have decided that he did not care what O'Grady did as long as he did not do it in Omaha. The young Irishman had a strong personality. I do know that even as an old man, after years of being a Washington power broker, O'Grady would occasionally mention a possibility that his enemies might conspire to fix it so that he would be called back to Omaha, a powerless provincial exile.

Headstrong and determined, he got to the University of Chicago's Sociology Department, then the best and most celebrated in the country. Sociology was not a subject Catholic priests of the period busied themselves with and to have gotten to a Baptist-tinged university that Catholics were discouraged if not prohibited from attending marked him as the accomplished finagler that he was.

There was much about O'Grady's life I never got straight. Who paid his tuition at the University of Chicago? How did he arrange the jump to Washington to become the church's lobbyist on many of the most important social welfare questions of the first half of the twentieth century? Once or twice I probed in that direction, but O'Grady would flash a twinkle and do a little verbal trickery which left me amused but ignorant.

He came over from Ireland the year Saul was born, a matter of mystical banter between the two of them. They believed that this coincidence was a sign, but of what I cannot say. The man himself was tall, sparse, with a theatrical brogue which some suspected he put on to coax and wheedle but I doubt it. O'Grady was sly, all right, but less of a charmer than an energetic, pugnacious battler inside his church with its ecclesiastic politicians and outside of it with Washington's secular ones.

It was O'Grady who along with Jack Egan had decided that I should meet Saul. Egan had no money himself and he was exhausting his contacts scrounging up money for the Latin American Committee. His hope was that through O'Grady, and ultimately Saul, a way could be found to put and keep the committee on some kind of sustaining basis.

At our first meeting O'Grady had looked at me through large blue, watery eyes and said, "Young man, you have fire in your belly. You should meet Saul Alinsky." I had no idea whom he was talking about, supposing it was someone named O'Linsky. But I was sure there was no fire raging in my lower parts, though he had sold Saul on the idea that I nursed a conflagration in that region. I was never able to convince either of them that my fires burned at a much lower temperature than theirs. I've always suspected that the reason Saul saw me as a younger edition of him-

self that first night when Egan and O'Grady took me to meet
him at the Palmer House Grill was because O'Grady had been
telling him I had fire in my belly.

Like Saul, O'Grady had to deal with the difference between
the idealized Catholic Church and the real one. He is quoted as
saying, "I had been a priest for eight years and I was 30 years old
before I realized that the Church was corrupt. It put me in agony.
I thought, 'What am I going to do? Shall I leave the priesthood,
shall I go out and become a doctor or a lawyer? What shall I do?'"
Then he is supposed to have answered his own question with,
"If I stay in the Church, at least here I'll have the word of God.
I'll have the example of Jesus Christ, I'd have Jesus Christ on my
side . . . but in the other institutions I wouldn't. So I decided to
fight it out on this line. I'll never make it to bishop, but I might
become a monsignor."[1]

When I was around O'Grady he kept God out of the conversation. I did not hear him use that kind of religious language but,
regardless, he had to wrestle with the same contradictions Saul
did, the difference between what institutions and people adver-
tised themselves as and what they were. When Saul and I were
with the monsignor the discussions were about projects, politics
and exchanging intelligence. Occasionally Saul sent me out of
town with O'Grady with orders to "make sure O'Grady says mass
on Sunday." We feared that the priest's casual approach to the
observance of his faith's ritual obligations might be discovered
by his enemies. Of course, by the time I met O'Grady he was an
elderly man, old enough perhaps to do something that might get
him retired against his will.

To protect him as O'Grady grew older Saul would boss him around but with an affectionate voice. Once at the Palmer House Grill, O'Grady was ordering a steak when Saul interrupted to tell the waiter, "No, he doesn't want that. Give him the white fish." "I don't like fish," O'Grady announced. "You know that, Saul." To which Alinsky replied, "For God's sakes, John, it's Friday. You can't be seen in a restaurant in this town eating meat on Friday." (The quotes are not literal but close enough.) Moderns have no idea the repercussions of a priest's eating meat on Fridays. The popes had laid down the rule and there were many Catholics who thought ignoring the rule to be a mortal sin. Meat eating in public on Fridays may not have equaled the more recent scandals besmirching the Catholic clergy but this was an era when the discipline was so tight moderns would have a hard time believing it.

Fridays, meat and O'Grady was always a fuss. When a fish bone got stuck in the old man's jaw, he popped the dentures out of his mouth to help extract it. Saul and I and the people at several neighboring tables were fascinated, watching until Saul could take it no longer. And it was "For God's sakes, John" again and then "Do that in the men's room." On another Friday O'Grady got stubborn about steak for dinner so we trooped up to his hotel room and ordered room service. When the waiter knocked on the door with our steak dinners, Saul made O'Grady hide in the bathroom while the table was being laid. These contretemps took place in an atmosphere of such suppressed laughter it occurred to me that the old man was having Saul on. He was capable of it.

When I met O'Grady he was in his late sixties and no longer the hard charger who bargained with Harry Hopkins, Franklin Roosevelt's right-hand man, on legislation. He was not long back from one of his African trips where he had spent time with "the fetish priests" who he was convinced had a role to play in creating effective health services there. Appreciating the potential contributions of fetish priests was a turnaround for a man who had labored for the professionalization of social work in America.

O'Grady had been a major force in changing the Catholic way (or nonway) of doing social work. When O'Grady began his career there was little we would recognize as social work in American Catholicism. There was charity or what were called "the corporal works of mercy." Most parishes had a St. Vincent de Paul Society, a group of parishioners who collected money, food, clothes and jobs, if there were any, for their distressed members and distributed them according to their needs and what was available to give out. It was not a perfect model of a local democratically run self-help organization thanks to the power position of the pastor, but it was closer to such a model than what replaced it.

These parochial, clerically dominated enterprises run by amateurs were, thanks in no small measure to O'Grady, demoted or even done away with in favor of centralized downtown Catholic Charities, tightly organized institutions administered by professionals trained in schools of social work. The Irish priest from the University of Chicago had been in the forefront of the effort in the 1920s and '30s to establish schools of social work at Catholic colleges and universities, to institute standards of professional practice and substitute credentialed personnel for the uninstructed priests, nuns and laypeople who administered the thousands of St. Vincent de Paul Societies. Now near the end of his career O'Grady urgently hoped to bring the St. Vincent de Paul Societies back to play a central role.

Although O'Grady came to agree with and back Saul in his belief that change should come from the people themselves, he did not damn the social work practitioners as Saul did. He had, after all, been an important figure in their professionalization, though he was hoping to deprofessionalize them and make them servants of democratically governed local communities. Saul had a different approach.

His reaction to social workers was about the same as a dog's reaction to a rodent. His experience roaming places where academics seldom trod taught him that social workers, holed up in settlement houses or caseworking the desperate and distressed, were out-of-touch emissaries of powerful outside interests stained by Anglo-Saxon Protestantism. They and all their works were a far piece from ground-up, local democratic control.

He made exceptions for social workers of Jane Addams's stripe. Hull House, which she founded on the Near West Side of Chicago, was not, unlike most settlement houses, a foreign body planted in a community that wanted no part of it or the people running it. Addams died in 1935 and with her perished the figure of the fighting social worker seen on union picket lines and attacking slum landlords. After her, settlement houses came to resemble WASP Fort Apaches hunkered down in the middle of hostile Catholic immigrant territory. The caseworkers with their social work degrees whom Saul dealt with were in the eyes of their clients bureaucrats, persnickety rule enforcers and hoity-toity scolds who dispensed the kind of charity that humiliates its recipients. He used to quote a college classmate, novelist James T. Farrell: "A sociologist is someone who needs a twenty-thousand-dollar research grant to find a whorehouse." He would come to have a similar opinion of social workers.

Historian Robert A. Slayton gives this description of the relationship of the University of Chicago settlement house in the Back of the Yards and the people in the surrounding neighborhood:

> The Settlement House's funds were of alien origin. They came from Hyde Park, the home of the University of Chicago, which was snobbish, condescending, middle-class and Protestant, or from the very rich, the bankers and business leaders in far away North Shore suburbs like Evanston and Winnetka— worlds apart from the residents of Back of the Yards. Worst of all, some of the money came from the Swift and Armour clans themselves, the hated overlords of the packing plants. These companies had no influence over the institution's policies, but their presence on the list of donators was a powerful weapon for the Settlement House's opponents. Even the Settlement House's residents were outsiders. They had none of the social guarantees that went along with being part of a local group and stood outside the nationalistic system because they were not ethnics, but WASPs. . . . The Settlement House workers were, in fact, from different backgrounds than their immigrant clients.[2]

In the 1950s when Alinsky was involved in an ill-starred attempt to organize in the Chelsea district of Manhattan, he col-
lided with a settlement house which reconfirmed his opinions
of the social work profession. The Hudson Guild, another Fort
Apache–type WASP organization, betrayed the community to
open the doors to an urban renewal project, Penn Station South,
which resulted in driving out ten thousand lower-income,
mostly Roman Catholic residents.

With certain exceptions social work and workers were, as it
was Saul's wont to tell them whenever he got the chance, a load
of crap. He saw them as buttinskies who fostered a perpetual de-
pendence in those they were supposed to help. By keeping their
clients in a state of powerlessness they helped the politicians
manipulate their votes and assisted organized philanthropy in
its work of social control. They used longer words and had
fancier pretensions but in Saul's eyes most social workers were
rice-Christian missionaries. For him social work was a tool for
top-down management instead of bottom-up governance. Social
workers, as far as he was concerned, were white-collar Pinkertons, a name which in his era stood for rent-a-cops employed by
companies to spy on union activity, escort strikebreaking scabs
across picket lines and use sap, club and gun on union members
as the occasion indicated.

The social work profession reciprocated. I can't remember her
name but I do remember that the woman who headed the University of Chicago's School of Social Service Administration—I
think it was a Helen Somebody—carried on a feud against Alinsky, a feud which was taken up everywhere by members of her

profession. The simple act of walking into a social agency and introducing myself as an employee of the Industrial Areas Foundation could induce something akin to paralytic terror in the staff. Having the power to cause such a reaction simply by saying a couple of words gave me a happy tingle. There was in Saul and certainly in my coworker Lester Hunt and me a bit of the boy prankster. We got a kick out of watching prissy-pants people go flying off in hysteria. It was like playing Genghis Khan Jr. We had fun with this stuff and, as Saul repeatedly said, when it stops being fun, it is time to quit.

TEN

JACK EGAN KEEPS HIS HAT ON; COLONEL RILEY KICKS OUR
LAMB OUT OF CITY HALL; IVAN ILLICH; MAYOR DALEY RUBS
HIS HANDS; JOHN MCGUANE EATS HIS ICE CREAM SUNDAES;
EGAN TAKES ME TO A FOOTBALL GAME

Every spring for a period of years the rector of Chicago's Catholic seminary sent a small group of the most promising members of the graduating class to spend a few hours with Saul. Like
that long-ago banker cautioning Bishop Sheil, Saul would explain
to these young men that they would have to choose between being
priests or bishops, between practicing their faith or practicing real
estate. These talks were not lost on many of them who went on to
spend their lives working with minorities and poor people.

Jack Egan was one of those. In 1943 he heard Alinsky tell them
that "on the day you're ordained, make up your mind whether
you want to be a priest or a bishop. Everything else will follow."[1]
Jack, who was struggling academically, made up his mind. He
also made it through seminary, thanks to a teacher who told him

that the church needed priests who were good with people more than it needed priests who were good with Latin.

His father, an office worker with the streetcar company, had taught him to work hard and obey the rules. And Egan did, winter or summer striding out into the world wearing a fedora because Cardinal Stritch had said his priests must go covered in public.

The friendship between Egan and Saul began some years later when, at the suggestion of Catholic philosopher Jacques Maritain, Egan invited Saul for lunch—a corned beef sandwich eaten in his office. Saul, knowing the tastes of many clergymen, was impressed that they had not gone to an expensive restaurant. Egan was then working with the church's Cana Conference, a program set up to strengthen Catholic marriages. The conference, under Egan, reached its apogee in the Togetherness atmosphere of the 1950s, and it enabled Egan to make useful contacts in almost every parish in the archdiocese, as well as in cities across America.

The battles for ecumenical cooperation, racial justice and power for the powerless sucked Jack away from Cana and toward Saul. After Cardinal Stritch created an urban affairs office and put Egan in charge of it, Jack began his IAF fellowship. It was because of Egan that Saul once again began organizing in Chicago, as he had not done since the early 1940s. Saul may have been the teacher but Egan brought with him a near-miraculous Rolodex, resourcefulness and a determination to get things going. It was Egan who had gotten the Catholic Church to give Lester Hunt, Juan Sosa and me the ten thousand dollars which

funded El Comité Latino Americano in the Woodlawn section
of Chicago.

And it was Egan who went to Cardinal Stritch, introduced
Alinsky and proposed that in addition to the church's backing
El Comité, they should have Saul undertake a study of the whole
Hispanic situation in Chicago with an eye to helping the Puerto
Ricans. Lester and I, both now on Saul's staff, conceived for bet-
ter or worse the San Juan Day celebration.

It was decided in 1955—by whom I cannot recall—to bring the
existence of the incoming Puerto Ricans to the attention of city
hall and the rest of Chicago. With the assistance of the Puerto Ricans themselves, but also a swarm of priests and seminarians,
there was to be a coming-out party for the new arrivals which
Saul had me orchestrate. *Time* described the ensuing madness:

> Ten moppets showed up at city hall to present Mayor
> Richard J. Daley with a baby lamb named Felicitas, after the
> mayoress of San Juan, Felisa Rincón de Gautier. The lamb is
> not only the symbol of Puerto Rico but of the Chicago
> church's potent and growing organization of Puerto Ri-
> cans. . . . There were heaps of lechón asado (roast pig) and
> pasteles (meat cakes wrapped in plantain leaves). Blind-
> folded children laughingly broke piñatas, whacking away
> with sticks at the hanging earthenware pots that might con-
> tain candy or water; music vibrated whole city blocks, and
> there were dozens of mambo, cha-cha and rumba contests.
> For San Juan is the patron saint of the island of Puerto
> Rico. . . . Armour & Co. provided 500-odd pigs and the prize

for reaching the top of a well-greased pole was a color television set.[2]

I believe that I recall a smile on Saul's face when he read in
the papers that, out of fear that the lamb would pee on the car-
pet, Col. Jack Riley, Mayor Daley's press officer, threw the mop-
pets, the priests, the seminarians and the animal out of city hall.
The colonel was subsequently sent to the big house for an unre-
lated crime.

The significance of this goofy event was the presence of Msgr.
Ivan Illich, sent by New York's Francis Cardinal Spellman to
take notes and report back. Illich was so enthusiastic that the
New York ecclesiastics exclaimed, "Let's do it ourselves!" and
with that New York City's famous or infamous Puerto Rican
Day parade was born to the joy of some and the consternation
of others.

The cardinal, who looked on Spanish-speaking people as a pe-
culiar Catholic responsibility, was also concerned with the ever-
growing, ever-worsening racial situation in the city. At this time,
the year of the *Brown v. Board of Education* decision ending lawful
segregation in the South, a low-level race war smoldered in and
around Trumbull Park Homes, a housing project on Chicago's
far south side. Elsewhere, racial violence flared here and there,
even as the races lived more apart in Chicago than in any city
south of the Mason-Dixon line, where Tennessee-born Stritch
was raised.

This period was also the high noon of federally paid-for urban
renewal or Negro removal projects as they were called by African

Americans. The bulldozers were knocking down the homes of black people, even as the whites struggled to keep the refugees out of their communities.

No help could be expected from the politicians and no help was provided. It was the Catholic Church or nothing.

With its membership in the vicinity of two million congregants, the archdiocese was also the city's largest property owner, largest hospital operator and largest private social services provider. Its school system accommodated so many children that, were it to close, the public school system would have collapsed. Now the social and economic foundations of all this were shifting and the archdiocese had no idea what it ought to do.

It needed eyes and ears and someone to propose plans of action. For a time, until Father Egan was set up in an office for those purposes, the IAF and Alinsky did what it could.

Toward that end Saul seconded me to Cardinal Stritch for whom I was to gather political skinny, gossip and other bits and pieces of interest. I reported every couple of weeks. I would turn up early in the morning at the North State Parkway mansion which was provided for the diocese's archbishops. A nun would let me in and I would wait. The furnishings reminded me of the lobbies of 1920s movie palaces. Once I took a peek into the throne room where the city's cardinals, in their capacity as "princes of the church," formally received visitors. Unlike his predecessor Mundelein, I don't believe Stritch ever used it. He would come bustling into a smaller room preceded by the swish of his red-silk moire cassock and a gentle clink as his pectoral cross hit its buttons.

Our meetings were casual. He would say, "Now, Sonny, tell me what's happening." On one occasion I showed him what was happening. We went to the Twelfth Street Illinois Central railroad station so his eminence could see for himself the arrival of the midnight train groaning with African American migrants from Mississippi, Louisiana and Arkansas.

The cardinal was so repulsed by the first Mayor Daley's ways of doing business that he could not stand being in the same room with the man. Whenever possible he avoided the mayor, which resulted in some convoluted forms of communication between Chicago's temporal and spiritual powers. On a few occasions I was one of the convolutions. I remember conversations with the political boss who sat behind his desk rubbing his hands with such force that the patches of skin between his thumbs and index fingers had been turned raw from the friction. The topics of these conversations, which consisted mostly of me talking and him rubbing, concerned race and public housing.

I would warn him that his public housing program was a social shipwreck in the making. He would rub. I would say some more and he would rub some more. Between rubs he put control of public housing in the city in the hands of a person who was called Flop House Charlie Swibel.

One time Daley said, rubbing away as he spoke, that he was setting me up for a lunch with John F. McGuane, a lifelong buddy from his Eleventh Ward base. McGuane was Daley's utility man and general fixer of the unfixable. I was to meet McGuane across LaSalle Street at the Bismarck Hotel, where the pols of that era and at least one city hall reporter I knew of ate their lunches downstairs and had their nooners upstairs.

McGuane turned up dragging the big man—I've forgotten his name—from the Chicago Real Estate Board with him. We ordered lunch, which for McGuane consisted of alternating ice cream sundaes with martinis. Before we finished eating, the real estate man had opened his briefcase and pulled out a map of the city. Spreading it on the table, he asked me to a draw a line anywhere on the map past which I would promise "my people" would not try to live. I reported back that I thought we were all doomed.

Egan opened new doors. Without him I doubt that Saul would have gotten the money from the Catholic Church that enabled him in the late 1950s to launch the organizing drives which made him the continuing influence he remains. Many years later Tom Gaudette, whom Egan convinced Alinsky to hire, remarked that "Saul just loved Egan, loved him as a priest. . . . Saul knew what a priest was. . . . 'But there's so few of them around,' he'd say."[3]

From time to time Jack would appear to say that I had been working too hard and would take me off for recreation. Once it was a car ride to South Bend to watch a Notre Dame football game. Once it was golf with several of his laymen friends. After three or four holes I was released and told I could trot back to the clubhouse bar and wait for them. But he was always there at the important moments. He became one of the first voices of prominence to denounce urban renewal and its treatment of African Americans. As the archdiocese's spokesman for urban affairs, he went before the Chicago City Council to call the University of Chicago's slum-clearance program Negro removal. That performance made all the papers and won for him the condemnation of whites, liberal and conservative.

He was with me in the lead car of a bus caravan of several thousand African Americans headed to city hall to register to vote, an unheard-of act of civic cohesion in that era—blacks registering to vote without the assistance of the regular Democratic organization's precinct captains. We were being escorted by a squad of black police officers and were making our way down what is now Martin Luther King Boulevard when we were stopped by a line of well-armed white police. The black officers and the white officers stared each other to a standstill. We seemed to be teetering toward a racial civil war inside the police department when Egan, wearing his Roman collar, black suit and fedora, walked past the black officers and up to the white ones. After five or ten minutes the line parted and we went on our way to arrive at a city hall guarded by more police armed with submachine guns. This time the ward committeeman of the Fifth Ward was standing there. When I asked if the police planned to machine-gun the voters, he said, "I'm trying to get them out of here!" He did and with the help of special registrars the names were inscribed in the books.

When Cardinal Cody shut down Egan's work with Protestants, Jews and minorities and ended his community organization endeavors, Jack did not quit as had scores of other Chicago priests, chafing under a retrograde hierarchy. He stood by his vows, but while still sticking to the rules, he helped put together the first clergy union, the Association of Chicago Priests.

His early academic struggles had taught Jack that he did not have all the answers and made him open to new ideas. At the end of his life, in his eighties, he circulated a statement asking the Vatican to permit a married clergy and the ordination of women. "Why," he asked, "are we not using to the fullest the gifts and talents of women who constitute the majority of our membership throughout the world? . . . I realize that even to raise aspects of this question, I label myself a dissenter. Yet prayerful, responsible dissent has always played a role in the church."[4]

They have erected a statue of Jack Egan on the campus of DePaul University.

ELEVEN

SAUL'S LONG FRIENDSHIP WITH A FRENCH THOMIST
PHILOSOPHER; ALINSKY ON SELF-KNOWLEDGE AND THE
ANGRY ANIMAL BELOW; THE IMPORTANCE OF NOT BLOW-
ING YOUR TOP; TELLING MARSHAL FIELD IV WHAT AND
WHERE TO STICK IT

As close as Saul was to O'Grady and Egan, these two men of action, it was another Catholic, a man of inaction, with whom he had a wider and deeper relationship. That was the philosopher Jacques Maritain. "At the time of his death, Maritain was arguably the best known Catholic philosopher in the world," according to the *Stanford Encyclopedia of Philosophy*. "The breadth of his philosophical work, his influence in the social philosophy of the Catholic Church, and his ardent defenses of human rights made him one of the central figures of his times. . . . Maritain's most enduring legacy is undoubtedly his moral and political philosophy, and the influence of his work on human rights can be seen, not only in the United Nations Declaration of 1948 but, it has been claimed, in a number of national declarations."[1]

The two could not have been less alike. The Frenchman was a gentle person with a cloistered personality, yet, "in spite of the radical differences in their personalities and backgrounds, Maritain was immediately attracted to this truculent genius of social reform, and the two men recognized their profound intellectual affinities," writes Maritain scholar Bernard Doering.

> Whenever they met they spent long hours exploring the democratic dream of people working out their own destiny. Both accepted democracy as the best form of government. As Alinsky tried to share with Maritain his ideas about what it is to be a free citizen of a democratic society, about the right of free association of citizens to undertake action and organize institutions to determine their own destiny, about the necessity of community organizations as mediating structures between the individual and the state, structures that help government do what it is supposed to do, and as Maritain explained painstakingly to Alinsky his ideas about the distinction between the individual and the person, the primacy of the individual conscience in a religiously and politically pluralistic democracy, about the primacy of the common good, about the source of authority residing in the people, who accord that authority to the government that acts in their name, each recognized in the other a truly kindred soul.[2]

Although they met in the early 1940s and Maritain went back to France at the end of World War II, they saw each other as often as possible and exchanged letters for more than thirty years until Saul's death in 1972. Given Alinsky's raspy tongue and reputation, "spiritual" is not a word associated with him but matters of the spirit were an important part of the friendship between the American organizer and the French philosopher. This passage in an undated letter from the rabble-rouser reveals an Alinsky altogether different from the figure whose reputation played such a strange part in the 2008 presidential campaign:

> After I finished reading your letter I left my office and walked for some time thinking—I suppose you would call it meditating. Jacques Maritain you are so filled with love and humility and compassion for your fellow man that you annihilate my defenses of skepticism and cynicism of you know what. Your letter almost restored the feeling that swept me as [a] 13-year-old boy standing before the congregation in an orthodox synagogue and celebrating my Bar Mitzvah.
>
> Life is odd—that I should feel twice that there is a good and great spirit close to me—once in a Jewish synagogue and once from one of the greatest Catholic philosophers—who will in time be ranked with Thos. Aquinas. I can never be anywhere the person you are because you really love all people, and understand with a great wisdom. There are some people I not only do not love but hate with a cold fury that would stop at nothing. I hate people who act unjustly and cause many to suffer. I become violently angry when I see misery and am filled with a bitter vindictiveness toward those responsible. This is

not good and I know it. I know just as well that I shall continue to feel and act as I have.[3]

Every once in a while he would talk about the anger in him.
He made it sound as though he believed there was a cast-iron
door down at the bottom of his being, a door which must not be
opened. He was big on doors, tunnels and gateways, leading to
surprises you might not like. It may have been his fascination
with *Alice in Wonderland*, a book he returned to again and again
to extract a metaphor.

When he talked about self-knowledge, he visualized it as a de-
scent into the pit of your soul. The analogy he used was of going
down through a series of hatchways and the picture I was left
with was of descending the hull of an ocean liner. With each
door you got closer to the final source of self-motivation, of the
reasons you were in this work, until you came to the last door
down at the bottom far under the water level. That's the one
door you don't open, Saul would say. Behind it was the angry
animal without conscience shoveling coal into a fiery boiler. The
door must never be opened, the animal never released but at the
same time you must acknowledge you need the animal to feed
off its fury.

Saul did not think that everyone had an innermost core made
liquid by the heat of anger, but he knew he had it and that he
needed it. He also knew he couldn't allow it out to have its way
with him. He must have struggled with the need for the anger
and the need to control it when he was younger and a hothead.
When he said I reminded him of his young self, a person quick

to anger, I don't think he realized that it wasn't that I was quick to lose my temper but that I was good at theatrical displays of indignation. Nevertheless, since a part of our relationship was built on his conviction that I was a younger edition of himself, I believe that when he attributed this or that trait to me, he was actually painting a portrait of his youthful self.

I don't know whether there was a single incident which taught Saul to curb his temper or his self-examination sessions taught him the need to do so, but what he did talk and write about was achieving the cold anger that fosters calculated and measured action. He harped on it in general and repeatedly with me, convinced as he was that I was prone to stop thinking and start swinging.

Saul had such moments himself, although you could never be sure when he let go with a blast whether it was anger or policy. He was a past master at goading the other side to lose its cool. Others saw it as evidence he was an egocentric, narcissistic man who was so fascinated with himself that he was indifferent to or oblivious of others' feelings. "Abrasive," "arrogant," and "sarcastic" were the adjectives often used about him when he was alive and still are. On one occasion he let Marshall Field IV have it at the Tavern Club, an upscale Chicago businessmen's establishment. Number IV, heir to the department store fortune, was the son of Number III, who had backed Saul and been on the Industrial Areas Foundation board. IV was unlike III, who died in 1956, but, as the owner of two daily newspapers and much else, he was a power in Chicago at a time when the higher orders suspected Saul of organizing hundreds of thousands of criminally inclined Negroes whom he intended to let loose to commit unspeakable acts on the white population.

What he and Junior, as Saul referred to Number IV, got tangled up about I can't remember but I do remember Saul—he was wearing the tan raincoat he always wore and was standing near the headwaiter's station—looking at the owner of the *Chicago Sun-Times* and saying, "Marsh, you can take that newspaper of yours and shove it up your ass." Number IV, who died a few years later, choking to death after he had swallowed his own tongue, stared as Saul walked away. Then Saul turned halfway around as though struck by an idea. "And make it the Sunday edition," he added in a low growl, pushing his fedora further back on his head.

That incident took place in the late 1950s when Saul had begun organizing in the Woodlawn section of Chicago, a very low-income area where the housing stock ranged from okay to pretty awful. It was an area coveted by the abutting University of Chicago, which wanted part of it for expansion and the rest of it to raze and use as a barrier to keep those people out.

The fedora got tipped back another time when Saul and I were strolling on the Midway, the grassy boundary that in those days separated the University of Chicago from Woodlawn. We were accosted by Bruno Bettelheim, a professor at the University of Chicago and the author of a series of books which made him the best-known psychologist in the country at the time. Bettelheim raged at Saul, accusing him of organizing the dregs of society—criminals, "animals," drug addicts, rapists—and generally letting a scourge loose on decent white people. At length Bettelheim exhausted himself and stood silent. Saul looked at him with a little crooked smile on his face, puckered his lips, one of his mannerisms, and said in a low-key, quiet voice, "Bruno, you're full of shit" and walked on.

Saul undertook the Woodlawn project with no black organizers, only white blue-eyed me. The organizing situation boiled down to the neighborhood saying something like, "Well, here comes this extremely white guy in a suit and tie from some downtown white organization I've never heard of looking like a lawyer or somebody worse knocking on my door with a cock-and-bull story about getting together and taking on the world." Given the history of race relations for the previous three and a half centuries, the problem was how you get the people to trust you.

If you are known by your deeds, you may gain their trust but we had no deeds as far as they were concerned. The other way is to have the right enemies and nobody was better at that than Saul, who had been using the tactic for years. In the middle of the Depression he needled the Chicago Democratic machine into canceling the free-milk program for poor kids, thus bringing a national furor down on themselves, retreating in short order and losing the skirmish.

The majority of Woodlawn's population did not read a newspaper, but those who did read IV's *Chicago Sun-Times*, which was obliging enough to begin blasting our doings. Fifty years ago newspapers carried weight, so when people in the neighborhood saw the paper's attack they were impressed.

They did not immediately trust us or come running to sign up, but if this major institution, the mighty *Sun-Times* with no

black reporters, attacked us, people concluded we were important and powerful. That we were neither was of little moment
since in organizing as in other forms of political activity it's the
shadow you cast which people react to. You don't want them to
see the figure casting the shadow, lest they find out it is only
your hands assuming bunny-ear shapes in front of a spotlight.

Field was not a hands-on owner so he may not have ordered
up the paper's attack but telling off IV in such a semipublic situation was the kind of thing which buttressed Saul's reputation
as Mr. Narcissis. "Narcissistic" is one of the words which has
been used into meaninglessness, but it's true that Saul did have
a big ego and he needed every ounce or inch of it.

TWELVE

THE RISE AND FALL OF THE COMMUNITY SERVICE ORGANI-
ZATION IN CALIFORNIA; ORGANIZING WHERE THERE ARE
NO CIVIC GROUPS OR CHURCHES; BEING FINANCIALLY SELF-
SUFFICIENT; ACORN; ALINSKY'S OPPOSITION TO PRESIDENT
JOHNSON'S WAR ON POVERTY; BARRY GOLDWATER; SAUL'S
PESSIMISM ABOUT RACE RELATIONS; BOREDOM

As had happened with the BYNC, Saul suffered a wrongheaded democratic majority again with the Community Service Organizations in California, the hugely successful string of Mexican American organizations put together in the late 1940s and early '50s by Fred Ross and César Chávez under Saul's aegis.

The CSOs had prepared thousands for citizenship exams and gotten thousands more registered to vote. Thanks to their work the first Latino since 1879 was elected to Congress in the person of Edward Roybal. Mostly forgotten now, the CSOs were the seed corn for much of what Mexican Americans have accomplished in California. "In the pre–Community Service Organization days," a member told Alinsky, "whenever a Mexican-American had a problem, regardless of whether that problem was related to the police department or to various services concerned with streets, lights, health, education or no matter what, that Mexican-American was always referred to as the dog catcher. The post was always filled by either political party with a Spanish-speaking person. . . . Imagine, every time something came up which had to do with the city, we would have to go to the dog catcher. But not anymore."[1]

Organizing through existing clubs, associations, churches and so forth was the most expeditious way of gathering people together but it had its limits. In California clubs, churches and such were next to nonexistent. An organization of organizations would have been an abortive weakling. The Community Service Organization fell back on recruiting individuals through house parties, an organizing tool that Barack Obama would use so successfully a half century later.

The same situation obtained in some low-income black areas where only a very small part of the population belonged to formal institutions. Other expedients had to be devised such as organizing by apartment building or getting occupations such as the beauticians together; at one point we had the hookers working on fund-raising. Organizations erected on such foundations as apartment building units or hookers have a tenuous existence. Because they do not reach a stable state, they need new recruits and a permanent organizing campaign. If the organizing ever ends, the organization will evaporate, which may or may not be a good thing.

With the CSOs, every money-raising expedient, enterprise or initiative available to people with little money but much energy and imagination was tried: secondhand rummage stores, carnivals, local service centers which charged CSO members three dollars a year to help with their individual problems, especially those having to do with immigration. César Chávez, who cut his teeth under Alinsky, took a shot at driving a couple of trucks up to Oregon to buy Christmas trees. Standing in the cold nights waiting for customers took its toll on the volunteers until, according to one fellow organizer, it was only "poor Cesar out there night after night among those thousands of Christmas trees, freezing his ass off and nobody buying any trees."[2]

Few community organizations gain independence by generating their own income streams. Ideally, community organizations ought to be able to realize the anarcho-syndicalist dream of networks of worker-controlled enterprises to support the organization. So far, however, starting profitable enterprises in low-income areas has been unspeakably difficult. While I worked for Alinsky we racked our brains trying to crack that nut but couldn't. So, few community organizations are self-supporting. Many are underbudgeted from the start. Others depend on foundation grants, government money, an occasional gift from a philanthropist. Not a few have had short life spans, no longer than the outside start-up money to pay the organizers lasts.

A number of community organizations depend in part on annual dues from affiliated religious congregations. In the Christian tradition those churches are usually mainline denominations. A half century ago when Alinsky was alive those churches had packed pews and overflowing collection baskets. In the first quarter of the twenty-first century they are in decline, pressed for money, torn by quarrels and schisms and losing membership to agnosticism and energized evangelism.

ACORN, short for the Association of Community Organizations for Reform Now, has been exceptionally long-lived and energetic. Although it was begun two years before his death in 1972, Alinsky had no direct part in its beginnings but nonetheless it is often said that this sprawling nationwide organization with local chapters everywhere was inspired by him. Its cheekiness, truculence and imaginative tactical tropes have an Alinskyan touch but the organization's handling of money, embezzlement and nepotism would have drawn his scorn. Nor would he have been comfortable with the large amounts of government money flowing into the organization.

Although Alinsky is described as some kind of liberal left-winger in actuality big government worried him. He had no use for President Lyndon Johnson's Great Society with its War on Poverty. He used to say that if Washington was going to spend that kind of dough the government might as well station people on the ghetto street corners and hand out hundred-dollar bills to the passing pedestrians. For him governmental action was the last resort, not the ideal one.

He felt that when the government, via one or another of its poverty programs, put the smartest and most energetic on its payroll it made an independent civic life next to impossible. He would point out that it opened up avenues of social and political control that could be used by government to stifle independent action. In the worst case the thousands of government-paid organizers could be turned into police spies. Writers like George Orwell and José Ortega y Gasset, men of the Left, now seem chiefly read by conservatives but for Alinsky their thinking was central.

He feared the gigantism of government, corporation and even labor union. The hope of his life was democratic organizations which could pose countervailing power against modern bureaucracies. It was only in that way, he thought, that personal freedom and privacy could be maintained. He did not trust the courts and legal protections to preserve individual liberty. It had to be backed up by countervailing power. For him, as he would often say, it was the struggle of the little man against big structures.

For these reasons he was less than enthusiastic about much civil rights legislation, although he kept his misgivings to himself. Around the time of Barry Goldwater's run for the presidency he was contacted by the senator and the two men had at least one meeting. Goldwater or perhaps one of his people had heard of Saul and they wanted to see if there was some common ground. The conversation, he told me, was about Goldwater's opposition to pending civil rights legislation. Saul shared the conservative misgivings about the mischief such laws could cause if abused, but he told Goldwater that he should not morally and could not politically oppose the legislation unless he had a better idea himself. The country was blowing up over civil rights. To stand mute with nothing to offer except opposition to the one legislative proposal on the table was untenable. The one position that was inadmissible, Saul believed, was to stand aside and let the racial status quo remain unchallenged and unchanged.

Much of Alinsky's organizational efforts had been to achieve equal rights and equal power but, if it could not be done by voluntary citizens' organizations, he believed there was no choice but to run the risks inherent in clunky, even brutal, governmental action. The last twenty years of his life centered on making whatever contribution he could toward racial justice.

In private he was pessimistic about how much could be achieved. He once said to me that "black is the only problem green cannot take care of," meaning that although money can ameliorate practically every other difficulty, he had his doubts it could bridge the racial divide.

I wonder if Saul would have thought that Barack Obama's election was a sign that the chasm had been crossed. Though Alinsky's posthumous reputation in some circles is that of an amoral, realpolitik man, the living Alinsky dedicated himself to ideals he had doubts would be realized. But he kept his doubts to himself and did not allow them to slow him down.

If building an organization is difficult, holding off osteoporosis is harder and not so much fun. Alinsky was an organizer, a man at his best when the weather was at its worst. Maintaining was not for him and, though he tried with the California Community Service Organization, I think his attention wandered. As is the case with many innovative companies, the founder, the one with the drive and the imagination to erect the structure, frequently botches the job of running it year in, year out.

Both Chávez and Saul wanted the CSO to build on its successes by organizing farmworkers, but the CSO membership would have none of it. Too many had attained modest incomes and middle-class status to see a connection between themselves and those laboring in the heat and the clouds of pesticides picking lettuce.

Chávez left the CSO staff to start the United Farm Workers on its brilliant, brief and ultimately sad course. The CSO, bereft of any dynamic reason for being, subsided, crumbled and in the fullness of time was gone. Occasionally Saul and I would talk about starting a chain of community organizations across the country which would unite in an umbrella organization with national clout. Ignoring the practical difficulties, I cannot imagine Saul hanging in long enough to make it happen. Setting up organization after organization in cities across the country would soon have bored him and Saul had a low boredom threshold.

Speaking of why he lost interest in his study of the Mob, he told a *Playboy* interviewer, "After I got to know about the outfit, I grew bored and decided to move on—which is a recurring pattern in my life, by the way. I was just as bored with graduate school, so I dropped out and took a job with the Illinois State Division of Criminology, working with juvenile delinquents."[3]

I think the thought of sitting on top of a national organization depressed him. Saul understood power, he wrote about it, on occasion he had it and used it, but he did not lust after it. He understood what a burden power can be and there were too many other things he was interested in and wanted to do, not the least of which was to have fun.

I used to think he overestimated my talents because I made him laugh. He was also prejudiced in favor of people who were good at popping out ideas and though his ego was big, it never asphyxiated those around him. But his preference for wacky things and wacky people made him intolerant of grinders. After I had left the IAF when we would gobble on the telephone he repeatedly complained about one man in the IAF organization. The guy was a grinder, excellent at the work but a grinder. He threw off few sparks and was short on a sense of humor. I told Saul to get off his case; the guy was doing all the boring grinder things Saul hated and wouldn't do.

There was a momentary pause on the line before he agreed. After that there were fewer complaints, but every once in a while Saul would return to the subject until I finally pointed out that the man was not on the payroll to entertain him.

THIRTEEN

MULTIPLE SCHIZOPHRENIA; THE IDEAL ORGANIZER; RE-
CRUITING STAFF; THE PROS AND CONS OF COMMIES AND
CHRISTIANS; DIVISIVENESS AND ITS USES; WHAT TO DO
WITH YOUR CANDLE AFTER YOU LIGHT IT; ALINSKY'S INTU-
ITION ABOUT CÉSAR CHÁVEZ; SAUL FLUNKS HIS OWN TEST

T he trouble we caused and the attention Alinsky garnered had
no relation to the size of his organization. There were years
when the whole thing was him, his secretary Dorothy Levin, Fred
Ross, César Chávez and Dolores Huerta in California and in the
rest of the country it was Lester Hunt and me.

Until the last couple of years of Saul's life, when committees
in four or five areas across the nation were raising money to bid
for the IAF to come and organize, money was hard to come by.
Alinsky was loath to hire anyone unless he had raised enough to
cover the organizer's salary for two years or more. An organizer
who also has to scare up money for his own salary is doomed.
The wherewithal had to be deposited in the bank before Alinsky

would make a hire. Those of us who worked for him were paid with what money there was.

For Saul, the ideal organizer had to have attributes beyond emotional toughness and seven-day-a-week endurance. This person ought to be able to be at home with, understand and speak the language of people of every background—the guys in the pool hall, backhoe operators, people in both the ghetto and the green suburbs, older women in white shoes with rhinestone-studded glasses working in dingy restaurants, those in the counting house, women law school professors and CEOs. The ideal organizer, Saul said, was a multiple schizophrenic, by which he meant someone able to think as others do. The ideal organizer should be able to partake of the feelings of those who pray and those who do not, of those who are oppressed and those who oppress them.

An organizer who looks like a madman or -woman will not be taken seriously. Those who are taken seriously will be seen as dangerous and will themselves be in danger unless adept enough to keep from getting their blocks knocked off. There will be no job security, no career path and when an exhausted organizer decides to change professions it will not help to put "outside agitator" in the "previous employment" line on a job application. If you worked for Alinsky you were something of a marked person, which did not matter if you were like Fred Ross or César, who intended to be lifetime bomb throwers. I had other intentions and told Saul I was his for ten years and after that I would be on my way. I understood that by then I would be radioactive, a stigma I hoped to lessen by keeping my name out of the papers and my puss off television.

To want such a job you had to have the yen, the itch to be a troublemaker à la Alinsky. You had to have a need to bust things up and reorganize them. Sometimes Saul would say that we were not organizers but reorganizers.

A job of this description is not going to be filled by putting an ad in the help-wanted columns, and we knew of no orderly method for finding staff. Usually they found us, or else we discovered them in the places where we were organizing. Saul told me once he recruited a key person in a California Mexican American community by stopping to fiddle with his pipe. He and the man had been walking in the barrio down a long muddy, unpaved street, where children were splashing in the sewer runoff along the side. Saying nothing Saul knocked the dottle out of his pipe, refilled it, lit it, puffed and looked, puffed and looked until the man exploded at the scene in front of them.

(For the record I can't recall Saul with a pipe in his mouth. He used to tell me that guys who smoked pipes were slow-witted. The reason, he explained, that they have them is that when they are stumped for something to say in a meeting they gain time by lighting their pipes or cleaning them or filling them.)

Saint Paul was one of our study models. After God knocked him off his horse and he joined the ranks of the people he had been persecuting, he was transformed into an organizer—a subversive preaching sedition by going from synagogue to synagogue, splitting the membership and making off with a minority as the basis for his new organization. But it was that minority— those with the energy and fury of new and true believers—who were the kind of people an organizer depends on; change is a form of creative disunion and demands nervy people to pull it off. Alinsky sometimes explained to new organizers that if you organized 2 percent of the population—that energetic minority—you would have enough power to overthrow the government. Not that he had that in mind. But with that 2 percent a successful and powerful community organization could be established. Provided the organizers did not collapse first.

There is a contradiction for those who believe the people must rule through a democratic process: this kind of reorganization ignores majority rule and seeks instead to create dynamic minorities. The best tool for doing this is creating controversy. Anyone not able to stand the tension involved would soon show the strain. We had one organizer whose hair fell out.

In recruiting people Alinsky was in a situation similar to John L. Lewis's when he put Communists on the payroll to organize the workers in the steel, rubber and other mass-production industries. The Communists were the ones with the zeal and the intelligence for the work. In place of Communists Alinsky often hired Christians. It wasn't a policy decision. They were usually the ones who would work until they dropped and who did not flinch at risky derring-do.

Religiously motivated people buzzed around Saul as though he were loaded with pollen. I had nuns tell me that he was a saint and ministers explain that he was a "true" Christian. Despite his friends in the priesthood, Saul was uneasy around people who talked religion and those who talked about "commitment" gave him the heebie-jeebies. He saw their words as mawkish sentiments dressed in the language of faith.

Saul would sigh when he looked across his desk at two or three heroic souls with romantic ideas about poor people. He could sniff out the difference between unctuous prattle about poverty and those with the naif idealism which blinds them to the actualities. The latter he took pains not to quash, although some of them could be so impractical. They came to him hoping to grapple with poverty through efforts like the Christopher movement, which teaches its adherents that "it's better to light one candle than to curse the darkness." Whenever Saul was told about that candle he would say with descriptive gestures, "It is better to take that candle after you have got it lit and stick it under the rear end of a corporate CEO or a slum landlord or a mayor. Light has to be applied to the right place."

Though it wasn't for him personally, Saul was not antireligious, far from it, but he understood the duality of religious institutions and the people who ran them. On the one hand there were the oft-proclaimed principles: sympathy for the poor, for justice, etc. On the other hand cash flow had to be considered, along with the hundreds of millions of dollars tied up in real estate—churches, schools, hospitals and other brick-and-mortar edifices whose value and utility were contingent on such things as the ethnic composition of the areas where they sat and with the physical blight which was spreading as rapidly as the polar ice cap was shrinking.

Edward Chambers, who at Alinsky's death succeeded him as the head of the Industrial Areas Foundation, seemed to have an opinion of his erstwhile boss almost as harsh as Alinsky's enemies, but the two men really did not care for each other. Nonetheless, Chambers' judgment has been that of many others: "I started forcing myself to look at what our kind of organizing meant to people. We worked with people in the churches, and their language was the language of the gospel. Their language was nothing like Alinsky's language. His language was power talk. Tough, abrasive, confrontational, full of ridicule. And those are really non-Christian concepts."[1]

Chambers had been a Roman Catholic seminarian and then had worked for Dorothy Day, the lay Catholic pacifist and apostle of social and economic justice. Saul, the secular agnostic, knew that every so often he had to administer a kick in the pants to some of these people of faith lest they turn an organizational drive into a tent meeting or a Salvation Army soup kitchen. If the danger with Communist organizers is that they may sacrifice the members for the cause, the risk with religious organizers is that they may sacrifice the cause to save an individual member, hearkening as they do to the words of Luke 15:7: "I say unto you, that likewise joy shall be in heaven over one sinner that repenteth, more than over ninety and nine just persons, which need no repentance."

Unfortunately, organizing demands concentrating on those ninety-nine.

In one lower-income African American community where the work of organizing was just getting under way in 1961, the members of the local businessmen's association were persuaded to provide Thanksgiving baskets. To the dismay of some, the organizer insisted that each basket have tucked in with the turkey a bottle of expensive name-brand Scotch. He explained that these baskets were destined "not for the needy, but the necessary," not for poor families who could use a luxury basket of vittles but for janitors and superintendents resident in the area's run-down apartment buildings where many of the tenants did not have telephones. The supers were the communication link to the tenants for everything from mass-meeting mobilizations to getting out the vote.

Although the truly poor would have welcomed that basket with or without the hootch, an organizer's job is to organize. Social work or charity is a draining distraction unless it can be used to recruit or strengthen the organization. Heartrending cases of sick people without decent care, innocent people marooned behind bars, children in worthless schools, old people snookered by mortgage brokers are of no interest unless they can be used to build the organization. With organization comes power and with power comes the possibility of helping the sick, springing the innocent from the jailhouse, finding jobs for the jobless or giving succor to the old people. When the organization is up and running, the baskets can go to the needy.

The people whom the janitors roust can be organized once they learn the ropes. Outside of the army most poor people, particularly if they are members of quashed minorities, have no experience with large organizations. When they do come up against them—the welfare office, the hotel or warehouse where they work, the hospital emergency room, box stores or the criminal courts—they are not running the machine but merely serve as low-ranked workers, clients or customers. In the past they might have learned how such organizations are run through contact with political machines or unions but these for all intents and purposes have vanished.

Among the stream of religious people, Protestant and Catholic, was Bob Squires, who had been recommended to Saul by Jack Egan. Squires was an African American Catholic from Cape Girardeau, Missouri, and unusual in not being an ex-seminarian. Squires was hired for the Woodlawn project, which would bring Alinsky as much attention in the 1960s as the Back of the Yards Council had twenty years before.

Religion also brought Ed Chambers to the IAF. He had been given the boot from the seminary for being mouthy and "after that," he wrote, "I hitchhiked from Iowa to New York City to Dorothy Day's Catholic Worker House. I was broke and hungry after four days on the road, and I found shelter at Friendship House, a Catholic interracial commune operating in Harlem in the 1950s. They had a storefront service center on Lennox Avenue and 134th St. That's how I stumbled into public life."[2]

I enjoyed teasing Chambers, telling him that although small, the IAF was an organization, not a commune, and that he would be paid by check, not by being given first pick in the secondhand clothes room.

Saul was doubtful about people with such backgrounds but like Lewis he did not have much choice. He might have drawn from a large pool had he been able to attract Jews with their tradition of combat for the underdog but they did not show up. Saul would wonder if some of his Christian job applicants were kooks or individuals whose talents would be canceled out by an inability to keep a rein on their evangelistic impulses.

One he worried about was César Chávez.

I remember Alinsky's coming back from a California trip where he had informed César that he was giving him a raise. César had refused it: the money should go into the work. Saul had argued with him, saying César had a family and children, but the refusal troubled him. Saul was a man whose enjoyment of the creature comforts ruled him out as an ascetic, religious or secular.

Though the saintly César later emerged to cast a spell over men like Bobby Kennedy, women like Dorothy Day and a wide liberal public, he was not a figure Saul could trust. The leadership he admired and whose decision making he could rely on was that of a Franklin Roosevelt or a John L. Lewis, men who might be devious, cynical, power loving and glory seeking but who lacked that pious tick that can make for calamity.

Alinsky believed that César didn't have the internal dialogue that keeps one aware of the outside world and puts life in perspective. A person who did not know and understand his appetites was someone, Alinsky believed, who lacked the self-knowledge to control himself or know what he was doing. Yet Saul helped César get seed money to start the farm workers' union, hoping it and César would end well. Neither did.

By the time of his death César had destroyed the union he had once led with such brilliance, leaving the Mexican American farmworkers as unorganized and defenseless as they had been before his rise. As the union reached its summit of accomplishment Chávez grew autocratic and dangerously eccentric. He fell under the influence of Chuck Dederich, the boss of

Synanon, a semicriminal drug-rehabilitation cult. Synanon's central rite, which César made his own, was the Game, in which a person, or in this case one of the union's staff, was put in the center of a room and surrounded by his or her colleagues who screamed epithets and accusations until the victim was reduced to human rubble. By this and similar acts of sadism the United Farm Workers' talented and dedicated staff was one by one driven off and the organization shattered by César's cruelty. The history of the farmworkers' tragedy is not well known but is well told by Miriam Pawel in her book *The Union of Their Dreams: Power, Hope, and Struggle in Cesar Chavez's Farm Worker Movement.*

Mary Beth Rogers, writing after Saul's death and relying on interviews supplied by some who worked for him, wrote:

> By the early 1960s, Alinsky had trained almost a dozen organizers on projects in more than a dozen cities. But he couldn't hold on to them. Organizers burned out or became disillusioned with the hectic lives they were required to live: always on the road, constantly overworked, underpaid, under siege, and most importantly operating with little or no direction from Alinsky, who acted as a Lone Ranger whenever it suited his mood. For the organizers, it was always start and start over. Very few organizations survived when the organizers left town for a new venture. . . . Alinsky was 56 years old and had become the guru of organizing in the United States. But he was tired. . . . Alinsky breezed into town periodically to advise on strategy and talk with the

press. Alinsky spent less time organizing and more time becoming a celebrity—a talker rather than a doer.[3]

No doubt about it, Saul was a talker but in those last years his
talking was also doing something. He was spreading the belief
that taking part in the decisions which affect their lives was the
right of all, that no people should be forced to accept the political guardianship of those who, by virtue of their wealth, feel
they can decide for others. Saul preached uppitiness for those
at the bottom: he preached the obligation people have to question, to be pushy and, if necessary, to be raucously disagreeable
and he explained how you can do those things. If America is a
less docile society than it was when Alinsky began his career
long ago, Saul is one of the reasons.

Even after I left him to go peddle my papers elsewhere, Saul
and I saw each other as often as we could and talked a lot on the
telephone, mostly about what the IAF was doing. If he did not
know what was going on in fine detail, he had me fooled. But
there is a grain of truth in some of the other criticisms. Saul did
get a huge kick out of being a celebrity but he used his celebrity
to propagate his belief that democracy is a proactive process.

The complaints which Rogers passes on from the IAF staffers
of that period, that Saul wasn't around much, wasn't giving
enough advice and wasn't himself organizing, have a certain justice if looked at from one point of view. Yet the genius of a good
organizer is getting other people to do the organizing. One person or two people are not going to be able to organize large num-
bers. The organizer's job is to find a few people in that mass

waiting to be organized who will do the job for them. Saul was a master of getting others to organize. If Saint Paul or Vladimir Lenin or Sam Adams had tried to organize on a one-to-one basis, there would be no Christianity, no Communism and no United States.

I was grateful that he wasn't around a lot. He would turn up with a reporter who was doing a story about him and the work and keep the press entertained and out of our hair. When you have media people on-site, everybody wants to be famous. You also run the risk that the reporters will notice that your organization is not nearly as big, as cohesive and as strong as you wish it were. With Saul doing his mesmerizing fandango, the media got to see and hear only what we wanted them to know. He and they would drop in for a while and then he would lead them off somewhere for a drink and fill their heads with visions of a better and greater tomorrow, allowing us to stumble on out of the spotlight.

Such infrequent visits were good, but if Saul had started coming around more often it would have driven everybody nuts. He was the big-picture guy, the man who could be called when something special was needed. I kept him closely informed by phone or memo and at critical moments he gave advice or, very rarely, direct orders. He expected independent judgment from his people.

His organizers were not well paid but to say that they were overworked is to imply that organizing then was a normal white-collar job. It wasn't. The times were turbulent, the work closer to bronco busting than to office work. Saul knew what organizing was like before it was professionalized into something close to a respectable, tenured occupation. In the 1950s he described his work to a meeting of the National Conference of Catholic Charities in St. Louis: "Nights, days, meeting in homes, lodge halls, church meetings, persuading, persuading and persuading in a constant fight against apathy and the feeling of anonymity of 'we don't count, nobody cares for us and there isn't much we can do about it.'"[4]

What Alinsky did then, what he thought of as community organizing, and what is done now, often in his name, are akin but not closely akin. Today community organizing is a recognized profession which people go to school to learn. Professional community organizers are paid decent money and often have health insurance and 401(k)s.

In one of his puckish moods Saul talked the president of a university into letting him anonymously take an examination being administered to candidates for a doctorate in community organization. "Three of the questions were on the philosophy of and motivations of Saul Alinsky," writes Saul. "I answered two of them incorrectly."[5]

FOURTEEN

SAUL'S OFFICE; THE IRS'S YEARLY DROP-BY; GEORGE P.
METESKY; THE THINKER; A SPECIAL PAPAL BLESSING

S aul's office was a small two-room suite at 8 South Michigan
Avenue. Built in the late 1920s Willoughby Towers was still a
prestigious address in the 1950s. The building had the respectability
which Saul needed when he moved in toward the end of the Great
Depression. A good address made the nascent Industrial Areas
Foundation seem like a member of the business community. It was
the same reason he called his one-man organization a foundation.
The word suggested substance, propriety and paid-up membership
in the status quo. Later on, Saul delighted in being a radical bogey-
man of national proportions, but when you are starting out, one
man alone with little money harboring upsetting ideas, the radical
tag makes it easy for others to quash you.

He had the office at a minimal rent because the building manager admired Saul. The man's name escapes me but not his
looks, smallish, bald, very pleasant, Jewish, I think, with a smile
and a twinkle. Although he never said anything directly, the

manager liked to give the impression that he, too, was part of the conspiracy of the little people, one of Saul's confederates. The building's owners apparently had no idea that they were supplying office space at a steep discount to the city's most dangerous radical.

People like the building manager were always popping up to tell me that they knew who I worked for and, though they might not find it convenient to get up in public and acknowledge it, they were with Saul. He was the champion of what they believed in and knowing that one of his followers might make himself known at any moment at any place kept me on my good behavior, which meant keeping my natural cynicism in check.

One of the most surprising figured in a story Saul loved to tell. For seven or eight years in a row the same IRS auditor showed up with his briefcase to go through Saul's records, both the IAF's and the personal ones, with the punctilio of his calling. It was slow going in Saul's cramped office space, because Saul was a demon about following the rules. Every expenditure had to be receipted and accounted for as necessary to our work. The boss had seen too many politicians and union officials knocked off or blackmailed because they played fast and loose with money. Every year Saul and the IAF passed the audit without a problem

At the conclusion of what, I believe, was the last of the interminable audits, as the IRS guy was packing up his things and putting them in his briefcase, he stopped, looked at Saul and said, "Mr. Alinsky, I hope you understand, these audits are not personal. It's just political."

Saul understood.

Saul's office was not furnished to impress. He had a few pictures on the wall of men he was close to. There was Marshall Field III and Gordon Clapp, the head of the Tennessee Valley Authority in the late 1940s and early '50s, and then a picture of a well-dressed man in a double-breasted suit with the kind of face you think you might have seen before.

Saul would ask a visitor if he recognized the man. Could he guess who he was? Most said he was a senator or a big-shot businessman. Nobody guessed that it was George P. Metesky, "the mad bomber" who terrorized New York City from about 1940 through the mid-1950s by planting pipe bombs in public places, particularly movie theaters. Exactly why George had his place of honor on the wall I cannot say. I think it was partly puckishness on Saul's part, partly a reminder that you don't judge a book by its cover or leap to conclusions. Saul had a strong Talmudic streak that came out in simple, vivid illustrations of the lesson of the day.

Screwed onto one wall of the office was a blackboard. When I first saw it I thought perhaps it was where we would plot strategy like generals going into battle, but to this day I have no idea why it was there. I never saw him pick up the chalk but once, way back when the board was new, and Saul carefully block-lettered his organizational equation: "Low Overhead = High Independence." It was one of the basic tenets of the Alinsky life credo. Keep it simple and keep it cheap. Never put on the dog; do not spend a dime on front or flash. And he never did. The least expensive, the most utilitarian furniture, the lowest rent, the fewest paid staff was his invariable rule.

At his desk, Saul had a high-backed executive armchair, nothing ostentatious, and there were a couple of wooden chairs for visitors. Delegations of more than two ended up standing or sitting on the floor. His desk was a grand clutter with heaps of papers, manuscripts, unanswered letters and memos, a clumsy, double-jointed florescent lamp and, Saul's favorite, a miniature of Rodin's *Thinker*. Occasionally he would indicate that if I were smart enough I should be able to extract wisdom from it. Once I asked if it would help if I rubbed my hand on the Thinker's back. I got the look and a "No." He said he didn't want me to wear *The Thinker* out.

Once looking at the unholy mess on his desk, I suggested we at least tackle the unanswered letters. I might have muttered something about crisp administration. Saul answered that the Alinsky method was to leave the pile alone until an alchemical process caused the unimportant stuff to take care of itself and vanish. Whatever was left he would deal with. It worked. Everything needing to get done got done.

There was one other thing on his desk. A key which had its own history.

In the late 1950s Jacques Maritain, who had been the French ambassador to the Holy See and still was a layman with much influence in Rome, arranged for Saul to meet with Giovanni Montini, then the cardinal archbishop of Milan. They were worried about the increasing grip of the Communist Party on the population of the Italian industrial North.

They hoped that Saul might come up with ideas on how to reverse this rising tide without reinforcing the reactionary elements who had less interest in democracy than in squelching the working man. Saul stayed in Milan for a week or so and, from what he said on his return, seemed to get on with the archbishop, who was destined to become the next pope. When the time came to say good-bye Montini said Saul ought not to leave Italy without having an audience with Pope Pius XII.

The archbishop arranged it and though Saul's audience was not a private one, the group was small. He was escorted into the reception room with a gaggle of pious American Catholics. I don't remember Saul's saying whether he genuflected to the Holy Father as his companions must have. The brief audience was concluded with each of his visitors extending a rosary for a papal blessing. Saul, of course, had no rosary, but he didn't want to appear impolite. Digging into his pants pockets he found the latchkey for his apartment in Chicago and held it out in the pope's direction. The key was duly blessed and earned a place of distinction on Saul's desk at 8 South Michigan.

FIFTEEN

SAM ADAMS, TOM PAINE AND ALINSKY; THAT WORD "RADI-
CAL"; WHY HE WROTE BOOKS; ALINSKY POLITICS VERSUS
ELECTORAL POLITICS; AMERICAN MACHIAVELLI; ALINSKY IS
DISCOVERED BY THE FEBRILE QUADRANT OF THE RIGHT;
NEW TACTICS FOR CHANGING TIMES

S aul's career spanned years of strife and change: the Depression, the McCarthy period, the civil rights battles and then the
tumults set off by the Vietnam War. (He did not play a part in the
antiwar movement, but on the night of the 1968 Democratic National Convention when the Chicago police lost it and clubbed and
beat the demonstrators in front of the Hilton Hotel, Saul was there
on the front line, facing the cops.) People with acceptably sized
egos, the kind which foster doubt and hesitation, do not have the
nerve and the decisiveness to do what Alinsky did. He died in 1972
before the expression "warm and fuzzy" had been coined, about
the time that America began settling into its prolonged, contented
coma from which it is just now emerging. Saul was a child of a
harsher time.

He, like the long chain of organizers who came before him and whom he believed would follow, understood that as often as not people look on their plight as incurable. They are reconciled to living next to an establishment putting nitric acid into the air; they accept working for pennies because that's the way things are. He saw himself as an heir to troublemakers going back to Sam Adams and the Boston Massacre. The citizens of the commonwealth needed to see that the British were not an unshakable burden but a load that could and should be cast off.

Saul wrote with a wire brush in the tradition of Tom Paine, whom he immensely admired as he explained in a letter to Jacques Maritain concerning his first book, *Reveille for Radicals*:

> Every stage of the book has caused fury and indignation even in the University of Chicago Press—a great part of the Trustees were completely opposed to publication of this book as being "radical and dangerous." One of them made the remark, "This is the filthiest piece of writing since Tom Paine." Each step of the production of the book has involved conflict. Marshall Field & Company are the biggest department store and seller of books in Chicago and had scheduled an autograph party for January 19. They have subsequently retracted their invitation on the basis that "this book is far too inflammatory and will be very disturbing to the morals and equilibrium of our employees." Marshall Field & Company, by the way, is noted for paying their employees less than any other similar establishment.[1]

Pure glee and pure Saul. He did so love to get the stuffed shirts hopping up and down. In the same spirit Alinsky kept the word "radical" in the title of his last book, *Rules for Radicals*, which may not be selling as well as *Common Sense* does but, though published more than thirty years ago, sells thousands of copies every year. Saul used the word "radical" because words such as "liberal" or "progressive" brought to mind logy, timid people who dared little and did less. Better to be thought an extremist than a do-nothing talker.

Saul wrote *Reveille for Radicals* to propagate the ideals and ideas which grew out of the organization of the Back of the Yards Council. I don't think he would have conceded it, but I think he wrote *John L. Lewis: An Unauthorized Biography* as an homage to a man Saul believed had played the leading part in bringing a dignified, decent middle-class life to millions.

Writing *Rules for Radicals* was a literary stoop labor for Saul and it seemed to me that he was at it, on and off, for years. He would call up once in a while and read me his newest aphorism which he had buffed to succinctness. Three decades later right-wing readers would glom on to them and make those aphorisms their own. Even while detesting Alinsky as a Marxist, they compare *Rules for Radicals* to Sun Tzu's *Art of War*, although I imagine Saul would have identified himself with another ancient Chinese philosopher, Lao-tzu, who is supposed to have said, "A leader is best when people barely know he exists, when his work is done, his aim fulfilled, they will say: we did it ourselves."

The book was intended as a teaching tool but it was written by somebody who had little expectations that organizing could be learned from a book or in a classroom. Nevertheless Saul hoped it would be used by people who had decided they were not going to be kicked around anymore. Thick with clichés as it may be, it has had a lasting impact. As for the clichés, Saul felt they were the clearest, most forceful way of getting his points across. He wanted to write for the masses à la Tom Paine and when I would tease him by pointing out that Paine was a superbly powerful stylist, not a clichémonger, Saul would put on a pouty face and walk into his office.

During his life Saul was accused of being Machiavellian, which pleased him because it made opponents nervous and nervous opponents make mistakes. It also pleased him because he knew that people calling him names was an indication of his effectiveness—besides, he basked in the attention.

He would have been tickled had he known that forty years after his death he would have graduated from being called Machiavellian to becoming the American Machiavelli thanks to *Rules for Radicals*, which seems to be finding a place on bookshelves and the Internet as the American version of *The Prince*.

It happens that Saul, who had read Machiavelli's other books, believed that the infamous Florentine was a democrat, an ethical man but a practical one who took the world as it was, not as he might have wished it to be. *The Prince* lives on and so it appears does *Rules for Radicals*. Its advice is not for princes but for ordinary people who want to make themselves heard.

People of many political stripes are taking a second look at him and the book, partly because of the imputed influence he may have had on the thinking and tactics of Barack Obama. Saul would have been doubly pleased in being awarded a part of the credit for electing a president.

Some of his critics have said that Saul was indifferent to electoral politics, but it is not so. He called a chance to go with a possible presidential campaign a chance to take a swipe at "the brass ring." He recognized its limits, however, and after studying Gandhi, watching Martin Luther King and working with John L. Lewis, he was convinced that people out of office and out of the electoral system can often get more accomplished than those who are hampered by being in it.

Outside of electoral politics, troublemakers and agitators have continued to consult *Rules* since it was first published. It may have less appeal for people who have gone into community organizing as a professional occupation than for those who fling themselves into organizing of any kind out of passion and anger.

Rules has much to teach community organizer professionals who are not comfortable with controversy but it may be most valuable for organizers in strife and crisis. In the past couple of years right-wingers have taken to carrying the book into battle. They are buying *Rules* by the thousands, which should be making Saul happy wherever he is, and are using it as their "playbook" after adjuring each other to skip the parts containing its nonexistent Marxism. A book entitled *Rules for Conservative Radicals,* presumably purged of Alinsky's wicked ideas, is out with a cover similar to the one on Saul's.

The tea baggers and other frightened and economically squeezed white-collar groups rely on *Rules for Radicals*. In the summer of 2009 many of them all over the country disrupted meetings on health care sponsored by Democratic members of Congress. They used *Rules* to get themselves organized and out protesting against President Obama's people who had, the year before, leaned on the same book, or at least the author's ideas, to get elected.

It has not been easy for right-wingers to pick out what they think they can use from Saul's work without being contaminated by the irreverence, but they hold their noses, say their prayers and fasten on the parts of Alinsky's prose that do not upset them. "What I think of Alinsky is that he was very good at what he did but what he did was not good," quoth Dick Armey, the former House of Representatives Republican majority leader speaking of the tea baggers' taking tactical lessons from Saul. "What's sauce for the goose is sauce for the gander," he added.[2]

Saul used irreverence as a tactic as he did in the organizing drive in Rochester, New York, where he divined that the company was run by stuffed shirts; a few years later their inability to change when faced with the dawn of digital photography would nearly bring the company down.

Alinsky was picador in the political corrida and irreverence was his banderilla. He enjoyed shaking up stuffy people who were blind to the twinkle in his eye when he carried on about how, like John Milton, he admired the Devil. That the Devil was the most perfect of angels did not impress Alinsky, who admired him for attempting a revolution and for preferring being free and being number one in Hell to being number two in Heaven. Like Don Juan in George Bernard Shaw's play, Saul conceived of Heaven as a rest home for bores; Hell was the salon where the interesting people spend eternity.

It is astonishing that anyone can read *Rules for Radicals* and not realize that its author was consumed by the demands of ethics. The first half of the book is a treatise on how men and women of action, people who do not shun power or its uses, can be both effective and ethical.

His was a topic that moral theologians of the last century with its mass murders, atomic bombs and concentration camps wrestled with. Alinsky was a rare, maybe a unique, ethical teacher because he was a man from the trenches who spoke with the benefit of experience which professors and ministers of religion ordinarily do not have.

His language distracts from the ethical side of his work. His words and phrases are harsh, pungent and provocative. That is as it must be because he was sounding the trumpet blast for democracy.

He put the word "reveille" in the title of his first book because he wanted to wake people up, but some of his readers get sidetracked by Saul's plain speech. His frequent use of the word "radical" came not from bomb-throwing revolutionary schemes but from a desire to make a distinction between those who talk a good game (liberals mostly in Saul's estimation) and those who play one (radicals).

"Rubbing the sores of discontent" is not the same as rabble-rousing. To say don't rub the sores is tantamount to saying don't do anything about the pain, accept it, learn to live with it, accommodate yourself to the way things are.

Rules for Radicals is not an ointment for those sores, an all-purpose salve for healing political carbuncles and social cankers. It is a book of principles to inform, not a cookbook to serve up the meal. Writing about *Reveille for Radicals* and *Rules* Alinsky said, "For some time after the book was published I got reports that would-be organizers were using this book and whenever they were confronted with a puzzling situation they would retreat into some vestibule or alley and thumb through to find the answer!"[3]

Some readers with more anger than sense skip everything and go to the tactics chapter. Saul had an imaginative genius for tactics, but he knew that tactics without organization are high jinks. Whether elaborately plotted schemes or noisy PR stunts, anything without a thought-out rationale was useless. Ego gratifying, perhaps, but useless.

He used to say, "Let's suppose you do it and let's suppose it goes just as you want it to, that step A works as planned and step B works as planned, you still have to answer the question, 'What the hell have you got?'" A one-day publicity splash, a rally or a sign dangling from the George Washington Bridge. To Saul, without follow-up and a larger strategy you've got nothing.

The most often-quoted may be rule 13: "Pick the target, freeze it, personalize it and polarize it." Thirteen is used as an example of Saul's ruthlessness, but no campaign can be won by attacking impersonal abstractions such as Injustice or High Taxes. The American Revolutionists personalized "no taxation without representation" by going after George III. Abstractions are not going to get feet marching. You must name who is responsible for it or those who are will slither out of reach with bromides like, "There is enough blame to go around." As Alinsky wrote, "The problem that threatens to loom more and more is that of identifying the enemy."[4]

The fifth rule states that "Ridicule is man's most potent weapon."[5] None could administer an infuriating jibe better than Saul but ridicule which only your side hears and laughs at is useless. Ridicule must reach the ears of the opposition to goad its leaders into angry overreaction and without organizational support to back it up, the humor is wasted. Otherwise ridicule, funny as it may be, will turn you into a stand-up comic and the people the jibe was intended to goad into a misstep will carry out their plans undisturbed.

"Never go outside the experience of your own people" is rule 2 and one Alinsky did not tire of repeating.[6] He had another way of saying it, which he did not put in the book: "If you get too far out in front of your own people you look like the people standing on the side." And another which I loved, although you might call it a contradiction to rule 2: "If you get too far out on a limb, keep crawling until you get to the next tree."

Saul was amused by his own inconsistencies because they caused some people to splutter, but he also believed life is inconsistent. He wanted to stress that in action there are surprises, and there are too many inexplicable events for internally consistent statements. Winners are not hampered by awareness of their inconsistencies. They bend their efforts toward studying the political topography, toward grasping the situation as it is. Winners recognize and seize on their advantages. Luck, Alinsky would tell you, is worthless if you aren't smart enough to know you have it and quick enough to use it.

Saul could turn on a dime. If the circumstances no longer obtained, he would jettison long-held, old ways of organizing. He foresaw the whirlwind which would take hold of the nation several years later with the 1963 March on Washington. The event which caused him to scratch approaches he had been using since Back of the Yard days was the civil rights meeting. We had organized it expecting that we would be lucky to draw fifty people since up to that time a civil rights meeting in the community could be held in a claw-foot bathtub. Instead, almost a thousand people appeared. Within hours Saul was on the phone to me, saying that we must have a completely new approach.

Toward the end of his life Saul decided that society had changed so much that new patterns of organization would have to be invented. Community organizing as he had once done it had, he thought, a limited future. It is sometimes said of him that he confined himself to organizing in a geographically defined community, but in the early 1970s just before his death, Alinsky had sniffed out the decomposition of community life as he had once known it and used it as a basis for organizing. "To organize a community," he wrote, "you must understand that in a highly mobile urbanized society the word 'community' means community of interests, *not* physical community."[7]

"I do not think the idea of geographical areas, especially neighborhoods, is any longer applicable," he said.

> A long time ago, probably with the advent of the car, we came to the end of the definable area. People no longer live their lives in neighborhoods. We have political subdivisions

which are things out of the past, lines on the maps, we are still involved with this idea. But the life of the people is something else. We are going to have to find out where it really is and how to organize it. . . . The whole point, I suppose, is to find out where the real interests of the people are. . . . They are not in what we habitually call the community. I do not think we know what the community is now. I find people running all over the country organizing on my principles. They were good principles but maybe they do not mean anything any more.[8]

Were Saul alive now he would not be organizing as he did seventy years ago in the Back of the Yards. He early saw that the America he had known in the days of a dynamic labor movement was fading into a white-collar world. He had seen the United Mine Workers with more than four hundred thousand members shrivel. He knew that their president, John L. Lewis, had not fought the introduction of labor-saving equipment or blinded himself to the decline of the industry; instead, Lewis had tried to find a path on which to lead his members into a changed existence.

Before his death, Saul had already begun to experiment with new approaches. Instead of picket lines in the battle with Kodak, he used stock proxies. Given Saul's vulnerability to new toys he would not have put up a technophobic resistance to the Internet. He was a sucker for every new office machine which came down the pike. Were Saul alive, he would be blogging and tweeting with the best of them.

Who he would be organizing and around what are more important. Believing as he did that every generation must invent its own forms of freedom and power, Saul would have attempted to help the atomized and unrooted white-collar millions find power and firm ground to stand on.

I guess that he might have returned to his own first beginnings, to juvenile gang warfare. He was not one to be daunted by danger. I can see him thinking in terms of organizing neighborhoods to smother gang violence and then taking a further step in doing something about public education by organizing parents, not simply to protest the shortcomings of the local public schools but to grab back their children from the grips of commercial media and electronic nonsense in all its forms and to motivate children to learn by controlling life at home and in the neighborhood.

He would be considering how to bring home to the national government the primacy of saving people before saving megabanks. He would have been toying with ideas such as seeing if he could assemble a squad of sixty or eighty top-flight organizers to move into a small-size city devastated by unemployment, house evictions and factory closings. A city such as Lorain, Ohio, or Richmond, California. The object would be to organize the entire community, everybody from top to bottom, to do something so dramatic it would hold the attention of the nation for days, something such as all the people marching on Washington. Then he might discard the idea as impractical but he would be working on something else. He would be at it night and day.

In the absence of a living and breathing labor movement, he would have been trying to invent new forms of organization so that workers, blue collar and white, would have a seat of power where their economic well-being is decided. I know he would have been troubled by the divisive rise of ethnic and religious groups struggling against each other to get more out of the government and becoming more dependent on the same government in the process. Saul had little use for the hyphenated-American idea. A reflection of Alinsky's thinking is apparent in the tens of thousands of people of Mexican background in California whom the Community Service Organization taught English and citizenship so that they became American-Americans.

SIXTEEN

WHEN SATYAGRAHA WORKS AND WHEN IT DOESN'T; RUB-
BING THE SORE; CHANGING TACTICS; WHERE MARTIN
LUTHER KING WENT RIGHT AND WHERE HE WENT WRONG;
THE USES OF VIOLENCE; EXPUNGING THE COMMUNISTS

S aul liked to use Gandhi as an example of a leader who perfectly
matched his tactics to the circumstances—tens of millions of
people too poor to conduct an armed insurrection against their
British masters. The only weapon they had was their ill-clad bodies
which, if located in strategic places, could bring down an empire
by simply sitting down. Mass satyagraha Gandhi knew would work
because, having lived among the British, he understood his opponents and therefore knew they would not act as Belgian King Albert
did in the Congo, where the killing did not stop until the subjuga-
tion was complete. It was in Saul's estimation a perfect analysis of
the circumstances matched to exactly the right set of tactics for
them. In that sense it was a perfect example of the "Alinsky
method."

The people Saul alarmed the most were the people who had the most and were most used to the unrippled life. A small stone skipped across their smooth waters got them imagining an inflamed mob and they pictured Saul as looking like Lenin at the Finland Station. If there was one thing Saul and Lenin had in common it was knowing that the point of "rubbing raw the sores of discontent" is not to get people running through the streets with Molotov cocktails but organizing for well-thought-out collective action.

Saul would point out that a winning tactic depends on the other side blundering into the trap you set for them. He used to give the example of what happened in 1961 when Martin Luther King took his campaign into Albany, Georgia, and the other side refused to respond as it should.

King's past successes had been due to his segregationist opponents' reacting to his presence by clubbing people over the head with nightsticks, setting dogs on them and so on. In Albany he came up against a southern sheriff, Laurie Pritchett, who cut out all the rough stuff and meticulously obeyed the laws as they applied to King's nonviolent demonstrators. In his own words Pritchett described how he was ready for Dr. King's nonviolent assault:

> We would book them, fingerprint them, mug them, put them on buses and ship them out. We never did what they intended to do. And King's philosophy, you know, was on Gandhi's, the march to the sea where they just filled the jails to capacity, and no place to put them, and then you've got

to turn in to it. Our plans had been made where we had the capability of 10,000 prisoners, and never put a one in our city jail. They were to be shipped out to surrounding cities that were in a circle. And we had fifteen miles, twenty-five miles, forty-five miles on up to about seventy miles that we could ship prisoners to.[1]

Despite the marchers' being dispersed in distant jails, treated decently enough so that there would be no martyr stories for the nation to shudder at, the civil rights leaders did not change their tactics. They kept on sending more people to be peacefully arrested and trucked off until the local movement had exhausted itself and King, lacking a better idea, had to take his operation elsewhere in hopes of finding sheriffs and police chiefs less tactically adept than Pritchett. And he did find them in Birmingham and Selma, Alabama.

Saul admired King's accomplishments, although he did not exalt satyagraha as the tactic to be used at all times and places. The metaphysical qualities attributed to it by King flew past Saul's ear, but he did not have to accept satyagraha as a quasi-religious credo to respect its utility. He knew that the black violence of the 1960s was suicidal and therefore, regardless of the provocation, witless. Satyagraha made sense to Saul because, as he pointed out when the subject of the gun-happy Black Panthers came up, African Americans were badly outnumbered in this country should race relations ever, God forbid, come to such a pass.

As with so much else, for Saul satyagraha was not a way of life but a tactic. "Take Gandhi," he said. "Even within ten months of India's independence, he acquiesced in the law making passive resistance a felony, and he abandoned his nonviolent principles to support the military occupation of Kashmir."[2]

In the 1960s and after Saul's death in 1972 satyagraha of a sort was practiced by the tens of thousands of college students in the leaderless, anarchic anti–Vietnam War movement. It had no Gandhi and no King up front and it had no Alinsky in the background. King spoke at antiwar rallies where he was a star performer but not a guide or leader. To appreciate why his talents could not be employed you have to appreciate the nature of this strangest of twentieth-century social movements, if a phenomenon of such short duration should be called a movement.

Those too young to have seen it or been part of the gallimaufry of passions, factions and eruptions will have difficulty picturing the events of those few frantic and sometimes inspiring years. I think Saul would have liked to have played a part in the campaigns to get America out of Vietnam. He despised the war, but the nature of this mass protest left no place for someone with Alinsky's talents to make a contribution.

He did what he could in a political and cultural upheaval which was short on leaders in the ordinary sense and long on "gurus." The word "guru" itself, previously obscure and often used with mild contempt, became popular in the antiwar mishmash of comic-book Marxism, vegetarianism, heroic figures, Hindu holy men, some genuine, some perhaps less so, stoned hippies, Quakerism, midwestern idealism, pacifism, serious, thoughtful people and crazy people, back-to-the-earthism, Hobbitism, adolescent revolt, stern moralists and stern amoralists and, in the phrase of the day, sex, drugs and rock and roll.

Like the millions Gandhi mobilized in India, the rank-and-file antiwar protesters in America had no history of interest in politics. Contrasted with the civil rights movement which was not only about racial equality but about poverty, the antiwar movement was mostly a one-issue movement finding its unity not so much in ending the war as in ending conscription. Alinsky appreciated the motives of the young men scrambling to escape a war which had no connection to their lives and concerns. He sympathized with the thousands of college boys, their lovers and their families protesting from a self-interest dressed in the raiment of anti-imperialist idealism. That is what people do and what Saul had often helped them to do, but in the chaos of their passions organization played only a minor role and Alinsky's forte, after all, was organizing and tactics.

From an organizational point of view the movement was a quarreling swarm of factions spasmodically coming together to pull off the demonstrations which made the movement so visible to the population at large and so disconcerting to people in power. For that they did quite well without Saul.

Saul never, as far as I know, discussed violence in public or wrote about it, but he had studied and thought about it. In his early years working at the Joliet penitentiary, he had met and dealt with men who did violence for passion, perversion, power and money. He had been around too many violent men in the labor movement and in organized crime to pretend that for good or bad violence hasn't taken its place in a stricken world. Saul graduated from college about the time the Nazis were coming to power in Germany and giving the world a lesson in the application of physical force in politics.

He wrote and talked about power all the time as he tried to overcome the namby-pamby-ism of the liberals and reformers and the social conscience of churchgoers who wanted to change the world but shrank from the means of doing it. But when he spoke of power it was always in terms of vote power or money power or public opinion power, never violent power. The subject was too touchy and to bring it up was to invite misquotation and distortion. In private, though, he would say that violence has it uses.

He had viewed it as a possible tactic in certain labor strike situations in the 1930s and '40s, though I'm sure he would say that as a tactic today it would be absurd. But back then when the employers had no compunction about initiating violence against their employees, sometimes the judicious and measured use of the same made sense.

Saul had a lot to say in private about how hard it is to control violence. It is not like an electric wall switch to be flipped on and off. Judicious and measured, he would tell you, is quite a trick to pull off. People can get violent when it is a tactical disaster or stay cowed and quiet when one punch would do a world of good.

A labor organizer friend of mine told me about a strike in a western Massachusetts steel-fabricating plant in the early 1940s. The place was surrounded by pickets when a file of trucks bearing scabs, as replacement workers were called then, drove up. He knew if that first truck got through the line and delivered its cargo of workers to the plant, it would demoralize the pickets and probably crush the strike. The lead truck slowed as it came up to the line and stopped with its bumper almost touching the picketers. The driver blew his horn and the people on the line looked at each other and began to shuffle to the side of the road.

Another four seconds and the strike would have been busted. My friend tensed and then jumped up on the truck's running board, yanked open the cab door, grabbed the driver by the front of his shirt and pulled him out and down on the ground. The driver got up and ran off as the strikers swarmed the other trucks; a melee followed with strikers and scabs going at it. For one more day at least the strike was intact.

In discussing the uses of violence Saul would explain that no matter how successful a union organizational effort might have been, there were always a few workers frightened by the company or just frightened who would not sign up. They were the ones who would cross the picket line, and that could not be allowed, even if it meant conking somebody on the head.

Those were the tactics in the olden days when heroic workers battled swinish bosses and Roosevelt or Truman lived in the White House. In the first decades of the twenty-first century, there seem to be more picket lines for or against abortion than for higher wages and better working conditions. Against such pickets, head conking is highly unwise. Lesser kinds of economic violence such as factory or lunch-counter sit-ins he defended publicly, but so did Martin Luther King. These are acts which, if not openly violent, are designed to provoke violence.

Political violence is trickier since it directly substitutes brickbats for ballots, yet Saul believed there were times when it had to be used. He died before Nelson Mandela had achieved his unimaginable feat of turning out the apartheid South African government by nonviolent revolution. It had been Alinsky's opinion that only guns could do that. Closer to home, Saul told me of one occasion when he was involved in political violence in America.

It was late 1939 or 1940 after the signing of the Molotov-Ribbentrop Pact, the nightmare agreement for believers in democracy, an alliance between Adolf Hitler and Joseph Stalin, between fascism and communism. The day before the treaty was announced, the American Communist Party had been all out in favor of war against Hitler and the Nazis. The next day they flipped over, announcing an isolationist position and peace with Hitler, since the German dictator and the Communist dictator were now linked arm in arm.

The Communist Party line which had been in enthusiastic support of the democracies suddenly favored appeasing Hitler. In a matter of hours, the Communists who had been among Roosevelt's most ardent supporters became committed enemies. After Hitler double-crossed Stalin by invading the Soviet Union in the spring of 1941, orders again went out from a panicked Moscow and the party flip-flopped again, becoming prowar and pro-Roosevelt.

If people who have gone to school in recent decades think of Communists in America at all, they think of them as the victims of McCarthyism and political persecution. The events in which Saul was involved took place before Senator Joseph McCarthy and McCarthyism, back when Communists, often men and women with dual loyalty, were operating with hidden agendas.

Groups which they could not control, they paralyzed with disruptive tactics, filibustering and parliamentary sabotage. One of their tricks was to force meetings to drag on for hours into the night. The non-Communists eventually went home to bed, leaving the floor open for the Red contingent to form a majority.

Members operating under party discipline, sometimes openly and sometimes keeping their party membership secret, held key positions in unions and civil rights and other left-liberal organizations whose interests they frequently betrayed. African American novelists like Ralph Ellison in *Invisible Man* and Richard Wright in *Native Son* tell stories of how a basically white party exploited and abandoned the black man. John Dos Passos writes of party-member obedience in *The Big Money*, the last volume of the U.S.A. trilogy.

By the time I came along, the sun had pretty much set on the Communist Party in America, but in one organization we were infiltrated by a small group of them bent on wrecking a key meeting attended by five or six hundred. They were stopped not by argument but by the chair of the membership committee, a chap named Dallas seemingly thirty feet tall, who showed up that evening accompanied by several of his colleagues from a nearby pool hall, all of whom had absentmindedly brought their cue sticks with them.

SEVENTEEN

ALINSKY AND HIRING WOMEN; HELENE'S DROWNING;
STALKED BY DEATH; THE O'GRADY BIOGRAPHY; MORE
TRAGEDY; CONSOLING MYLES HORTON ON HIS LOSS; THE
RAGPICKER OF EMMAUS; IRENE

After his death, attacks and criticisms of Alinsky have persisted through the years, a tribute to his enduring relevance. Some come from community organizer professionals who do not think that he got it right, that he was too ready to fight.

He is accused of being antiwoman, of not hiring them as organizers. In fact, he did hire a few and didn't doubt that women could do the job. As far as I could tell, he thought women can do anything men can do. He took them seriously and was not a man to keep company with Kewpie dolls or trophy girlfriends. The four most important women in his life had professional careers.

Saul's reason for avoiding female organizers was simple. He felt that sex where you were organizing led to fights, divisions, cliques and aimless plotting. He was conditioned by union attitudes of the 1930s and '40s, which translated into apprehension that women organizers or pork choppers as union staff were often called were trouble. Saul did not think that they caused trouble but that when men and women were in close, stressful situations, working long hours together, sex would rear up and shake its lusty mane. He would tell staff, "Don't get laid in the community unless you are ready to lay everybody." His other caution was, "If you're going to shack up, don't do it within a hundred miles of the community." A blowup over sex was disorganizing. He thought it less likely to happen if the organizers were all of one gender. I don't think assembling an all-girl orchestra occurred to him.

> *That I shall never look upon thee more,*
> *Never have relish in the faery power*
> *Of unreflecting love;—then on the shore*
> *Of the wide world I stand alone, and think,*
> *Till Love and Fame to nothingness do sink.*
>
> —JOHN KEATS, "WHEN I HAVE FEARS
> THAT I MAY CEASE TO BE"

The worst thing that happened in Saul Alinsky's life was the death of his first wife, Helene. I do not think he got over it, not all over it, not even after he married Irene, his third wife with whom he was delightfully happy. I believe that Helene's spirit and her death stayed with him.

Dorothy Levin, Saul's secretary, told Sanford Horwitt, his biographer, that ten years after Helene drowned in Lake Michigan saving their daughter and another child, she opened the door to

Saul's private office before leaving for the day. He was dozing in his upholstered chair. "She gently asked him, 'Saul, is everything all right?' He, startled in the darkness, called out, 'Helene?'"[1]

He talked to me about Helene's death from time to time and spoke of death itself often. He told me that she died because somebody on the party-line telephone in the vacation area where they were staying would not get off the phone so that a rescue squad with a pulmotor could be summoned. Saul himself was many miles away in Chicago when Helene drowned. He declined an offer by a state trooper on the scene to find out who hogged the party line. He was afraid of what he might do if he had the name.

There were darker stories about what might have happened to Helene which I did not know what to make of. It seemed Saul could not accept that Helene, an accomplished swimmer who had taught Red Cross water rescue classes, could have perished as she had. In telling these stories he may have been schooling himself to a reconciliation with death itself. Death, not the fear of death, the fact of death, walked with him.

Saul would tell people how he visited Helene's grave until a cemetery worker explained to him he had been putting his flowers on the wrong marker, that she was not buried where he had been standing head bowed. The irony of weeping over a stranger's grave showed him the uselessness of his mourning. In that sad yet comic moment of putting roses where it made no sense, he came to believe in his own end. He also came to think in that graveyard that most of us do not believe in our dying.

He wanted me to understand that knowledge of our death is the key to living; he wanted to impress that upon me, but I was too young to take his meaning fully to heart. It was another case of his taking me to be deeper and more devoted to the ideals he served than I was.

Saul reminded me of the central figure in José Saramago's *Year of the Death of Ricardo Reis*, where it is written:

> It is difficult for one who is alive to understand the dead. I suspect that it is just as difficult for a dead man to understand the living. The dead man has the advantage of having been alive, he is familiar with the things of this world and of the other world, too, whereas the living are incapable of learning the one fundamental truth and profiting from it. What truth is that, That one must die. Those of us who are alive know that we will die. You don't know it, no one knows it, just as I didn't when I was alive, what we do know without a shadow of a doubt is that others die.[2]

After Helene's death, Saul was unable to get over his grief. He had ceased organizing or doing much of anything else. To try to free him from the paralysis that had begun to turn from months to years, his friends conceived a project which would bring him back to life. He would be asked to write a biography of his friend Monsignor O'Grady. It was to be called "Come Now, Monsignor," perhaps because of the disturbing tales Saul said it contained.

It was never published. Probably it was never meant to be. During the time I spent with John O'Grady, I got the impression there was nothing he wanted less than to leave the world with an account of what he had done or was witness to. O'Grady may have developed an aversion to saying mass, but he was still a churchman as well as a secular politician-lobbyist. He was less interested in tidying up the historical record than taking certain parts of it to the grave.

Saul never said anything about the biography's being a conspiracy of his friends. As he told it, the book was to contain descriptions of key episodes in the New Deal years. It was to be about the politics of progress, an insider's story about the social and economic policies which were to dominate the rest of the twentieth century and endure until they were pulled apart by the reactionary policies of a resurgent Republicanism.

O'Grady's political discretion was so great, according to Saul, that as each chapter of the book was given him to read, the monsignor scrubbed it clean of any historical or gossipy interest. The censored, mangled and unpublishable manuscript lived on a shelf in a closet next to Alinsky's door. Saul, who could have as touchy an authorial ego as the rest of us, treated the whole business as a joke and his relationship with O'Grady remained the same.

When his friend Myles Horton also lost his wife and also was immobilized with grief Saul telephoned Horton, insisting he come to Chicago to work on a grant application and report which would provide funding for Highlander Folk School, the training center for nonviolent civil rights actions. Saul told his friend that the deadline for filing had been moved up and the paperwork was due in just ten days.

According to Horton's biographer, Myles "went to Chicago and worked with Alinsky night and day on both the grant application and the report. The deadline came closer and closer, yet everything that Horton wrote Alinsky rejected. It wasn't what the foundation would want, Alinsky kept saying. Highlander was desperately short of funds; Horton had to finish and finish well.

"Finally, in the early hours of the day the foundation was supposed to meet, Alinsky told Horton that what he had written was acceptable and would be in the hands of a secretary in time." As Saul eventually confessed, the deadline had not been moved; the meeting was still weeks away. Saul, whose friends had roused him with John O'Grady's "biography," had done the same for Horton.[3]

Death came visiting Saul again and after that they stayed in close touch. A few years after Helene's death in 1947 he fell in love with another woman, but Babette Stiefel was struck down with polio, clapped into an iron lung and was dead a month later.

After Babette he did marry again, but Jean, his second wife, fell ill in ways that affected her emotional life. She became impossible to live with. I visited them in the little place he had bought for her in Carmel, California, and I did not see how he could stand it. She would move about kicking the furniture, yelling at him, throwing pots on the floor, grumbling, accusing him of neglecting her. She turned the little house into a little hell.

His friends would tell him that he had to separate for his sanity and that it was not disloyal. After what seemed to me too long a time, he got a divorce, but he did not abandon Jean. He would fly out to see her and supervise her medical treatments.

Saul wasn't a locker room guy. When speaking of sex his language was not crude. He favored semieuphemisms—get laid, toss in the hay, shack up, with the last the one he seemed to prefer. Sometimes he would call women dames in the manner of Humphrey Bogart, whom Saul knew.

Depending as he did on religious organizations for a large part of his budget made him even more anxious about any incident involving sex, though when one did occur it wouldn't have been the IAF which was embarrassed but the archdiocese. A French priest known as the Ragpicker of Emmaus arrived in Chicago, at whose invitation I cannot remember, but he brought with him a saintly reputation. A figure out of Victor Hugo's Paris, he worked among the poorest of the poor, those who lived under bridges and in the sewers, making what living they could finding and selling rags.

In Chicago the abbé turned out to have less of an eye for the destitute and more of an eye for the ladies. There followed a couple of opéra-comique days while Saul and Jack Egan, neither of whom spoke a word of French, tried to wedge the erring clergyman onto an airplane so that he could return to his homeland and attend to *les misérables*.

Saul seldom talked about marriage or sex with me. His views were conventional and I had the strong impression that he was faithful to his marriage vows. He liked women, he liked to flirt, but he wasn't a promiscuous personality. After he married his last wife, Irene, he had an apartment in Chicago and she lived in Boston, an arrangement that he would impart to whatever man he happened to be sitting next to on the airplane. He would describe with glee the envious expression on his traveling companion's face but that was Saul being Saul. He was so in love with Irene that he got mope-ish when he was on the road away from her—or so it seemed to me when we spoke on the telephone.

EIGHTEEN

SAUL'S YIDDISH MOMMA; THE WORMORATOR; PANG MAKES
THE FRONT PAGE; KARSH OF OTTAWA; A PATRIOT AGAINST
THE VIETNAM WAR; ARCHY THE COCKROACH

O nce a month, Saul would sigh and head off for lunch with
his mother. He tried to make it sound like an ordeal, but he
loved it as he made clear in a magazine interview:

> She speaks more Yiddish than English, but she collects all
> my clippings, even though she's confused about what I'm
> doing, and she gloats over the fact that I'm the center of a
> lot of attention. "My son the revolutionary," you know. Once
> I was the lead speaker at a mass meeting in Chicago and I
> thought she'd enjoy seeing it, so I had her picked up and
> taken to the auditorium. Afterward, I drove her home and I
> said, "Momma, how did you like my speech?" And she said,
> all upset, "That's a fine thing you did, to do a thing like that,
> what will people think of your mother, how will they think
> I brought you up?" I said, "Momma, what was it I said?" And

she said, "You don't know? You ask me, when twice, twice
you wiped your nose with your hand when you were talking?
What a terrible thing!" You know . . . what are her first words
to me on the phone? "Have you got your rubbers? Are you
dressed warm? Are you eating right?" As a Jewish mother,
she begins where other Jewish mothers leave off. To other
people, I'm a professional radical; to her, the important thing
is, I'm a professional. To Momma, it was all anticlimactic
after I got that college degree.[1]

Sarah lived in such a different sphere that she could not grasp
what her son did for a living but, as his name began to appear in
the newspapers, her pride in him grew apace. He was famous,
ergo he was successful. At one of their luncheons Saul, in an attempt to get her to understand what he did, compared it to the
Peace Corps, an outfit for which, incidentally, he had little use.
To Saul's delight, she asked what was it, this Piss Corps. Around
the office it became the Piss Corps, although Saul remained in-
capable of pronouncing the phrase with a Yiddish twist.

Saul had a weakness for gadgets. Hammacher Schlemmer, the
New York City store specializing in wacky widgets, was a death
trap. I think that is where he got the wormorator or whatever
the thing was called. He got back from New York one time and
showed it off in the front yard of his house in the Kenwood section of Chicago. With some difficulty he forced the instrument
into the earth and turned the electricity on, enabling its rays or
vibrations or beams or whatever it emitted to do their work. In
a couple of minutes worms were popping up through the grass

all around us. It would have verged on the horrifying had the worms been slightly larger but Saul turned the wormorator off, the worms wiggled back into the bowels of the earth and after a few weeks of astonishing unwary visitors, the wormorator must have been relegated to the back of a closet.

If the purpose of the wormorator was to get bait to hook bass it was news to me. The Saul I knew did not fish. I have seen pictures of him as a young man, standing against a rural background holding up his catch and that implied he had caught the fish, but I don't believe it. He told me that before I met him he had had several brushes with the outdoors and the results had not been satisfactory. Though at one time he played tennis, the only form of exercise I associated with him was walking. Sauntering, really, since that is the ideal pace and style of ambulation for the raconteur he was.

The only time I saw Saul walking rapidly was if it was raining. He took rain amiss, it being his belief that drops from above were, in his words, "God pissing on me." The remark was slightly out of character since Saul never acted as though he thought God or anyone else was persecuting him.

If the existence of the wormorator would have surprised those who viewed him as a dangerous bomb thrower, so would the presence of Pang. The name of this gigantic husky, Saul informed us, was Eskimo for "tough" or "rough" or some other frightening quality which those of us who met Pang attributed more to Chicago than to Alaska. It was Saul's second wife, Jean, who was responsible for Pang's presence in the house, but Saul was taken with the dog and boasted that when he and Pang went for a walk, people crossed to the other side of the street, fearing the animal which looked like a cross between a wolf and a polar bear.

Pang spent a fair amount of time at my house and his personality did not fit his appearance. I would come home to find wife and children strewn over the floors, knocked down by a happy Pang who was romping around the place, wagging his tail, his big red tongue out and a goofy expression on his face.

When a major blizzard buried Chicago, Saul called his friend Stuffy Walters, the managing editor of the *Chicago Daily News*, and persuaded him to send a photographer to snap Pang pulling Saul's car through the snow. And, heaven help everybody, the next day a picture of Pang among the snowflakes was on the paper's front page.

In many ways Saul was a conventional middle-class man, a non-bohemian like the non-bohemian masses whom he strove to organize. Like Mayor Richard J. Daley whom he bumped up against more than once over the years, he was a Chicago White Sox baseball fan, a committed one. He did not come to destroy the social order but to perfect it. Saul was comme il faut, neat with nothing sticking out or flapping in the breeze. He was as ruly in his person as he was unruly in public life. I never saw him without a shirt, a tie and a suit or a sports coat. His tie was kept where it belonged with a tie clasp, the bar kind that slides in place, not the tack kind whose pin risks damaging the material. He always wore cuff links.

His hair was a Brylcreem ad, staying where it belonged which took some doing because he was born with intensely curly-crinkly hair. It was the sort of hair that would have enabled him to sport what in the 1960s was called a Jewfro. To subdue it, when he woke up in the morning Saul wound hot towels around his head until the last kink had straightened itself out.

His revolution was political, not sartorial. Taken together, the shined shoes, the creased trousers and the neatly pressed look of a successful, conservative businessman served as a carapace against any suggestion that Saul had a connection with loose living, free love, pot smoking or any of the other habits that had been associated with the Left going back to the days of Emma Goldman.

Saul's radicalism was not of dress, manners or how people chose to live. Communes and social experiments were no concern of his. Lifestyle, a word I never heard him use, was of no interest. Individual liberty was a keystone to his credo, and how you lived was your business. But if you worked for him, how you looked was his. Hence his first instructions to me: get a haircut; buy a suit.

There were two things Saul wanted: to be on the cover of *Time*, which in his era was a very big deal, and to have his portrait made by Karsh of Ottawa. He didn't get the first but he did get the second.

In the middle years of the twentieth century, to have Yusuf Karsh take your photograph was attestation of fame and importance, even world renown. The Canadian photographer's study of Winston Churchill is the best-known and most revealing picture taken of the English war leader. I don't recall any advance negotiations, but when Saul got the call from Karsh he was off to Canada.

Some of Karsh's portraits seem to be their subjects' ideal visions of themselves. Franklin Roosevelt appears to be standing unaided, Alexander Calder is the maker of new art forms,

Vladimir Nabokov holds up a small picture of a butterfly, Muhammad Ali's is as much fists as face and a 1944 Charles de Gaulle appears to be bringing light out of darkness. The Alinsky portrait was pure Saul and he was delighted with it. Not a hair out of place, head slightly to one side suggesting sympathy, leaning forward a little to hint that he was, though pensive, capable of action. You can see one of his cuff links, and, as he had done with Picasso, Edward R. Murrow and Humphrey Bogart, Karsh posed Saul smoking a cigarette.

Out of the developing fluid Saul materializes, not as an organizational genius or an arch provocateur and master troublemaker but as a recognizable American male of the era. The American is important because he was patriotic. He was against the Vietnam War, but he had no use for the people at the antiwar demonstrations carrying Vietnamese flags. The antiwar types who jeered servicemen returned from the war disgusted him. He never got over seeing a soldier in the bar where Saul was having a drink. The man in full uniform was sitting alone weeping at the jeers that had met him on his return from the war. The incident was one of Saul's oft-told stories.

Saul delighted in causing trouble but his politics and organizational tactics were economical. He was not a troublemaker for the hell of it. When it came to the work his focus was matched only by his self-discipline. Sometimes he would imagine chucking a firecracker into the chicken coop for the fun of seeing the angry hens flapping in full squawk. He loved public fuss and feathers, but when it came to the work he practiced the politics of simplicity. No pranks, no idle tricks, no vengeance, no revenge, no feuds, no pride, no anger, no vain boasting, no side trips, no detours, no self-indulgence and no ego tripping.

He was a good boss. When there was nothing to be done, he did not expect people to be at the office pretending. My colleague Lester Hunt and I had a taste for nonsense around the office, inducing in Saul pseudoexasperation and laughter. When we were on our game he would carefully and slowly take off his glasses, laughing all the while, to wipe the tears away. His was not a roaring or a belly laugh. He laughed silently but when you got him going he could not stop. He was good with spouses, taking time to talk to them about the work. He even visited my mother, an indomitable feminist. "He's terrific!" she pronounced. Others have other views of him but to me at least he was a man of great kindness.

In slack periods with Saul there was talk about Alexis de Tocqueville, the Chicago White Sox, Socrates, Freud, Locke, *Alice in Wonderland*, Archy the cockroach, and his friend Mehitabel the cat and his shares of stock in Pocketbooks, given him by Seniel Ostrow, the CEO. For a while he was a paper-profit winner, but as I recall he waited too long to sell.

In the nine years he lived after I left the IAF employ we remained close friends. I had given him the ten years' service I had promised him and the fire in my belly, if it had ever raged, was now extinguished. My last day on the job, Saul rose from the high-backed chair behind his desk and we embraced and cried. I was the best man at his wedding.

One afternoon he talked about how he would arrange his own death. He had more than one death scenario. None involved suicide but he did believe he got to pick. One that he did not pick was a long, slow decline, a gentle deathbed with family gathered around. There would be no soft slipping off to any good night for Saul Alinsky. He would go to South Africa, join the guerrillas and die fighting to overthrow apartheid. He would know when to go to the airport and seek out the bullet meant for him. It would be a selfless death to equal Helene's.

I told him the guerrillas wouldn't take him with that eyesight of his and so Saul died on a sidewalk in Carmel, California, from a heart attack. It was fast. He wanted that most of all. But it damn near killed Egan and me and the rest of us who loved him.

NOTES

INTRODUCTION

1. Richard Wolffe, *The Making of a President* (New York: Crown, 2009). Stephen C. Rose, "Kos and Alinsky and Election 2008," *Huffington Post*, August 20, 2008; available at http://www.huffington post.com/stephen-c-rose/markos-moulitsas-zniga-sa_b_120091 .html. Noam Cohen, "Know Thine Enemy" (Word for Word/Saul Alinsky), *New York Times*, August 22, 2009.

CHAPTER 1

1. As quoted in John T. McGreevy, *Parish Boundaries: The Catholic Encounter with Race in the Twentieth-Century Urban North* (Chicago: University of Chicago Press, 1996), 10 (emphasis in the original).

2. Barack Obama, "Why Organize? Problems and Promise in the Inner City," in *After Alinsky: Community Organizing in Illinois*, edited by Peg Knoepfle, Illinois Issues (Springfield: University of Illinois, 1990).

3. "Ace Dies Martyr to Own Code," *Chicago Daily News*, October 5, 1927.

4. Marion K. Sanders, *The Professional Radical: Conversations with Saul Alinsky* (New York, Evanston and London: Harper & Row, 1965), 14.

CHAPTER 2

1. Barack Obama, *Dreams from My Father: A Story of Race and Inheritance* (New York: Three Rivers Press, 2004), 133.

2. Ibid., 229.

3. Michael Gecan, *Going Public: An Organizing Guide to Citizen Action* (New York: Anchor Books, 2004).

4. Taylor Branch, *At Canaan's Edge* (New York: Simon & Schuster, 2006), 467.

5. Saul Alinsky, *John L. Lewis: An Unauthorized Biography* (New York: Vintage Books, 1970), 145.

6. David J. Garrow, *Bearing the Cross: Martin Luther King Jr. and the Southern Christian Leadership Conference* (New York: William Morrow, 1986), 441.

7. Beryl Satter, *Family Properties: Race, Real Estate and the Exploitation of Black Urban America* (New York: Henry Holt, Metropolitan Books, 2009), 131.

8. Sidney Lens, *Unrepentant Radical: An American Activist's Account of Five Turbulent Decades* (Boston: Beacon Press, 1980), 93–94.

CHAPTER 3

1. Sanford Horwitt, *Let Them Call Me Rebel: Saul Alinsky, His Life and Legacy* (New York: Alfred A. Knopf, 1989), 320.

2. Arnold R. Hirsch, *Making the Second Ghetto: Race and Housing in Chicago, 1940–1960* (Chicago: University of Chicago Press, 1983), 147.

3. D. J. R. Bruckner, "Alinsky Rethinks Idea of Community," *Washington Post*, February 20, 1969.

CHAPTER 4

1. Saul Alinsky, *Rules for Radicals* (New York: Vintage Books, 1989), 46–47.

2. Hirsch, *Making the Second Ghetto*, 209 (see chap. 3, n. 2).

CHAPTER 5

1. Garrow, *Bearing the Cross*, 455 (see chap. 2, n. 6).
2. Ibid., 466.
3. Sanders, *Professional Radical*, 51 (see chap. 1, n. 4).
4. *Chicago Daily News*, January 26, 1966.
5. David Dawley, *A Nation of Lords: The Autobiography of the Vice Lords* (Prospect Heights, IL: Waveland Press, 1992), 108.
6. As quoted in Branch, *At Canaan's Edge*, 441 (see chap. 2, n. 4).

CHAPTER 6

1. R. D. G. Wadhwani, "Kodak, FIGHT and the Definition of Civil Rights in Rochester, New York, 1966–1967," *Historian* 60 (1997).

CHAPTER 7

1. Alinsky, *John L. Lewis*, 23 (see chap. 2, n. 5).
2. Ibid., 116.
3. "Meat and a Bishop," *Time*, July 24, 1939.
4. Horwitt, *Let Them Call Me Rebel*, 124–125 (see chap. 3, n. 1).

CHAPTER 8

1. "The Bishop's 25th," *Time*, May 11, 1953.
2. Donald F. Crosby, *God, Church and Flag: Senator Joseph R. McCarthy and the Catholic Church, 1950–1957* (Chapel Hill: University of North Carolina Press, 1978), 164.

CHAPTER 9

1. Horwitt, *Let Them Call Me Rebel*, 261 (see chap. 3, n. 1).
2. Robert A. Slayton, *Back of the Yards: The Making of a Local Democracy* (Chicago: University of Chicago Press, 1986), 175–176.

CHAPTER 10

1. Margery Frisbie, *An Alley in Chicago: The Ministry of a City Priest* (Kansas City, MO: Sheed & Ward, 1991), 30.

2. "Religion: Fiesta," *Time*, July 2, 1956, available at http://www.time.com/time/magazine/article/0,9171,891298–1,00.html.

3. Frisbie, *Alley in Chicago*, 121.

4. Peter Steinfels, "John J. Egan, Priest and Rights Advocate, Is Dead at 84," *New York Times*, May 22, 2001.

CHAPTER 11

1. *Stanford Encyclopedia of Philosophy*, s.v. "Jacques Maritain," http://plato.stanford.edu/entries/maritain/.

2. Bernard Doering, "Maritain in America—Friendships," in *Understanding Maritain: Philosopher and Friend*, edited by Deal W. Hudson and Matthew J. Mancini (Macon: Mercer University Press, 1987), 42.

3. Bernard Doering, ed., *The Philosopher and the Provocateur: The Correspondence of Jacques Maritain and Saul Alinsky* (Notre Dame: University of Notre Dame Press, 1994), 5.

CHAPTER 12

1. As quoted in P. David Finks, *The Radical Vision of Saul Alinsky* (Ramsey, NJ: Paulist Press, 1984), 65.

2. Ibid., 66.

3. *Playboy*, interview, March 1972.

CHAPTER 13

1. As quoted in Mary Beth Rogers, *Cold Anger* (Denton: University of North Texas Press, 1990), 98.

2. Edward T. Chambers, *Roots for Radicals: Organizing for Power, Action and Justice* (New York: Continuum, 2003), 93.

3. Rogers, *Cold Anger*, 89.

4. As quoted in Finks, *Radical Vision*, 80 (see chap. 12, p. 1).

5. Alinsky, *Rules for Radicals*, 169 (see chap. 4, n. 1).

CHAPTER 15

1. Doering, *Philosopher and Provocateur*, 22 (see chap. 11, n. 3).

2. Edward Luce and Alexandra Ulmer, "Obama Foes Turn to '60s Radical for Tactical Tips," *Financial Times*, August 16, 2009.

3. Alinsky, *Rules for Radicals*, 138 (see chap. 4, n. 1).

4. Ibid., 130.

5. Ibid., 128.

6. Ibid., 127.

7. Ibid., 120 (emphasis in the original).

8. *Washington Post*, February 20, 1969.

CHAPTER 16

1. Oral history interview with Laurie Pritchett, April 23, 1976, Interview B-0027, Southern Oral History Program Collection (#4007), Center for the Study of the American South, University of North Carolina at Chapel Hill.

2. *Playboy* interview (see chap. 12, n. 3).

CHAPTER 17

1. Horwitt, *Let Them Call Me Rebel*, 211 (see chap. 3, n. 1).

2. José Saramago, *The Year of the Death of Ricardo Reis* (San Diego: Harcourt Brace Jovanovich, 1992), 234.

3. Frank Adams, *Unearthing Seeds of Fire: The Idea of Highlander* (Winston-Salem, NC: John F. Blair, 1975), 80–81.

CHAPTER 18

1. *Playboy* interview (see chap. 12, n. 3).

INDEX